Martin R Oliver grew up in the industrial city of Coventry, England. He left school and worked in a car factory before joining the Merchant Navy. He later immigrated to Brazil but now lives between Dubai and Bangkok. He has previously published two books: a travel book, *The Never Lonely Planet*, and a book of short stories, *Worlds Apart*.

Martin R Oliver

Happy Jack

Reflections of Growing Up During the Sixties – A Decade of Rebellion, Change and Defining Moments

Austin Macauley Publishers™
London • Cambridge • New York • Sharjah

All of the events in this memoir are true to the best of author's memory. The views expressed in this memoir are solely those of the author.

A CIP catalogue record for this title is available from the British Library.

ISBN 9781528992022 (Paperback)
ISBN 9781528992039 (ePub e-book)

www.austinmacauley.com

First Published (2021)
Austin Macauley Publishers Ltd
25 Canada Square
Canary Wharf
London
E14 5LQ

Table of Contents

Preface

Dear Reader,

Happy Jack: *Reflections of Growing Up During the Sixties – A Decade of Rebellion, Change and Defining Moments* is a collection of my memories of growing up and coming of age, during that period, and those many tumultuous events which transformed the world.

Can anyone truly explain, how it was possible for a country and its people to change so dramatically in just ten years? London, suddenly transformed itself from a conservative capital city to one of the most vibrant, colourful and exciting cities in the world.

On both sides of the Atlantic, a catalyst of a youth cultural revolution spread throughout, creating social change, evident through its music, fashion, literature, art, innovated technologies and a young counterculture which challenged the establishment and questioned authority. A generation that believed that anything was possible.

Some denounced it as a decade of irresponsible excess, flamboyance and decay of social order, others refer to it as the Swinging Sixties.

I grew up in the industrial city of Coventry, which at the time, was being extensively rebuilt in the aftermath of the Second World War and re-establishing itself as the heart of the UK's car production industry. Jobs were plentiful and wages higher than the national average. Workers came from all over the country to find jobs in the factories and reconstruct the city. It was a time of social levelling, a time when industrial workers found they could earn enough to purchase televisions, refrigerators, motor cars and eventually own their own homes. I was blessed with a loving, caring family and wonderful friends and workmates. The experiences and fond memories of which, have remained with me throughout.

Martin R Oliver

Chapter 1
'Queen Bee Bar', Bangkok

People today are still living off the table scraps of the sixties. They are still being passed around – the music and the ideas.
Bob Dylan.

I am sitting in the bar, chatting with a few expats, when a guy leans over the table and asks me in a slow American drawl, "Martin, when you were young, were you a *mod*?"

I look at this guy and think to myself, *He is not that old, and he is American, did he say 'mod'*.

"I am sorry, did you say mod?"

"Yeah, I was looking at your hair style and manners, and it seemed like you would have been a mod when you were young."

Smiling, "Yes I was, but what the hell do you know about mod's, they were around in England during the sixties."

Again, in his drawled American accent, "Well my favourite movie ever, is *'Quadrophenia'*, about the mods and Rockers era, written by the rock band 'The Who', and you remind me of those mod guys."

Being retired and in my sixties, I was flattered.

An elderly English guy, sitting next to me, overheard us, and he got into an excited conversation with the American, describing the various soundtracks and music associated with the Quadrophenia movie.

My mind, in the meantime, drifted back to those days.

As I grow older, the one thing that I appreciate about my life, as much as anything else, is that I grew up in Britain during the sixties.

Chapter 2
Retire or Expire

I mean, some doctor said I had six months to live, and I went to his funeral.

Keith Richards.

There are stages in one's life that seem so far away – you just don't see them coming, but they do. It happened to me recently, when I finally retired after nearly fifty continuous years of work, in over three continents.

So, now, I find myself in another continent, '*Asia*', spending time and treading water (as they say) in Bangkok, a city which has become my second home for a number of years now.

Bangkok is an amazing city, where all kinds of people come to visit and decide to stay for many different reasons. It's a harbour for those that need shelter, for some when they feel they can no longer be loved or can find love, and others that are looking to create a new life for themselves. Elderly men from Europe, Australia and Japan come looking to re-invent their youth and feel like they are eighteen again, or to find a young Thai wife. There are the foreign tourists, looking to explore the temples, tourist sites and shopping malls, the sex tourists, looking to explore the go-go bars, shady massage parlours and nightclubs. Nationalities from all over come for the cheap medical and cosmetic treatments that this city offers. Many of those people become regular visitors, and for different reasons, eventually make Bangkok or Thailand their home.

Due to budgetary purposes, my dream of owning a boat, retiring in a house next to a river, and a golf course at some exotic resort, has instead been replaced by spending my days idling in Bangkok, a city renowned as on average, the hottest city in the world. Here, I pass the days, reading and writing, or exploring and walking the streets, dining on street food on the evenings, before visiting sleazy bars that sell cheap beer. Over the years, I have come to believe that Bangkok has the most interesting, eccentric and extraordinary expat community of any major city, and a lifestyle that is affordable and rich in culture.

My drinking partners, in and around the bars of Bangkok, are tourists looking for love, bargirls looking for lovers' money, lady boys and gay guys, back packers from all corners, expats like myself, who have settled or retired here, and those shady secretive strangers that one meets, those weird characters that only tell you half of their story, and leave you guessing as to their reasons and their past. Could they be the ones that leave home after faking their own deaths or are involved in some kind of insurance scam, or criminals hiding from the police, or absconding from a prison sentence wherever they may come from? Thailand is a sanctuary for liars and losers, and for the private detectives hired to uncover such characters, not to mention those hired by wives to follow and report on their husbands, who suspiciously find all kinds of reasons or excuses to visit Thailand far too often. It was Jim Morrison, the lead singer with the rock band "Doors" who said "I drink so I can talk to assholes. This includes me!"

For many people, retirement comes as a relief, with the freedom from working every day, time to play golf or do the gardening, and go shopping with the wife. Whereas for me, I am still growing up and learning about life. If I have learned one thing about retirement, it is to stay away from those type of people that complain about everything and nothing, those that wallow in self-pity by talking about health issues and their personal problems and ailments.

Health, rightly or wrongly, is something I never thought about before retirement, it was never an issue with me, but now I am in 'the zone', it's a subject that comes up in conversations all too often. I have learned things lately about aging that one really doesn't need to know.

Some old guy, sitting at the bar, recently, jubilantly explained to us, 'his drinking buddies', that once we have reached the age of 65, statistically we are generally good for another 19.5 years, but during that time we can look forward to a number of common health issues, such as arthritis, heart disease, cancer, respiratory diseases, and Alzheimer's disease to name a few, do you want me to go on? Well there's diabetes, pneumonia, depression, substance abuse, and even poverty! It's a slippery old road ahead, so my alcohol intake habit does not seem so bad, in comparison.

I believe the experience of growing up during the sixties' decade, together with my working-class upbringing and the simplistic lifestyle of that time, has left me appreciating the simple things in life, without getting sucked in to the materialistic, egoistic, corruptive world we live in today. Our younger years are where the seed of what we are, or what we will become, are sown. Yes, I can be grumpy and a little opinionated, but really, I don't give a shit. Why should I worry? I was told, after an interview with a careers officer that visited our school one day, that maybe I should consider a job in a supermarket stocking the shelves. I did better than that. I heard it said when I was young, that if I masturbated too much, I would go blind. I didn't take much notice of that either, and can happily boast that my eyesight is still good today!

Thinking about health reminds me of a medical check-up I had in Dubai (my other home and a complete contrast to Bangkok) a few years ago. I arrived at the clinic in good time with urine and stool samples and waited my turn to see the doctor, who turned out to be a pleasant English guy. He asked me all the usual questions about my health, like do I drink and smoke, took my weight, height, etc., before sending me off to the other departments for the chest x-ray, eye, hearing, and blood tests, before returning to him for a final examination. He studied the results, nodding with approval saying, "Okay, just strip off, and sit on the couch."

"Strip off?"

"Yes, take all your clothes off, relax and sit on the couch."

I did as he said, but the atmosphere in the room changed somewhat, when the doctor walked over to the window, looked out, and after a few seconds, said casually, "Sheikh Zayed Road looks very busy this afternoon, I wonder why!"

I shrugged my shoulders, and said, "No idea," thinking to myself, *What the fuck has the traffic on Sheikh Zayed Road got to do with the current circumstances*? being I, sitting naked on the couch.

I then watched him walk across to his desk, pause a second, before slipping a fine rubber glove onto his right hand. He looked at me and said, "I want you to lay on your side and put your knees up to your chest."

Well I did what he said, and it all happened very quickly, he carried out a prostate exam by putting his fingers as far as he could up into my rectum. He told me to get dressed and went on to explain that the prostate gland is around the size of an almond (or did he say olive), and it should be firm not too soft, and it controls this and that, all of which was going in one ear and out of the other, as I was in a mild state of panic.

I got dressed, and before leaving, I mentioned to the doctor that my mother died because of problems with her prostate. He gave me a very strange look, and said, "I very much doubt that she did."

I said, "I am quite sure she did."

He wished me a good afternoon.

I made my way to the cashier desk, and settled my account, without looking the cashier in the face, feeling guilty, as when I did, when I went outside into the street. I felt ashamed, like I had been misbehaving, and passers-by were looking at me with suspicion.

I walked slowly across to the car park, and as I was getting into my car, I remembered. My mother died because of complications with her 'pancreas'.

I wonder if that doctor still remembers me!

Chapter 3
A Different Generation

If there's not a rebellious youth culture, there's no culture at all. It's absolutely essential. It's the future.

John Lydon.

It has often been said that our sixties' generation, which grew up during that decade, have a better love of life, are more tolerant, less materialistic, and far less egoistic than later generations.

Significant cultural changes to daily and family life in Britain actually began during the nineteen fifties, as people's lives were getting back to normal during the years following the Second World War. The innocence, and sometimes simple way youngsters were entertained, taught and raised at that time, most certainly contributed to the personalities and characteristics of a younger generation growing up during the sixties' decade.

Comparing with youngsters of today and how they are raised, one wonders how most of us survived those years at all. There was no bottled water, we drank water from the tap, there were no warnings of lead poisoning from the domestic water pipes, and even many of our toys were painted with lead-based paint. Medicine bottles just had a cork stopper, no childproof lid. We had no fridge and food had no expiry dates. No mobile phones, so our parents couldn't contact us whilst we were out all day, exploring surrounding areas, stealing fruit, climbing trees, jumping streams, and getting 'soakers' (wet feet). Kids would build their own bicycles from any old parts they could find, and make trollies from a piece of wood, supported by wheels taken from old prams or pushchairs.

Bikes would always get punctures, and we had to learn to repair them ourselves.

We would arrive home tired and hungry, at the end of the day, just as it was getting dark, with bruises and scratches and torn clothes, all part of being a kid. If the local cop caught us breaking the law or misbehaving, he would take us home, and report us to our parents, who would normally thank him and give us a bit of a hiding. We didn't care, it was something to brag about. There were no fancy games, we had to invent them ourselves. Most of all we were allowed to be kids, to dream to invent and to play how we wanted. It is therefore no wonder that the generation that grew up during that time created some of the most innovative and exciting technology, music and humour we have today.

Today, we have become a generation of '*health freaks*', with a health culture greatly dictating our wellbeing by advertising, marketing, and our addiction to social media, a lifestyle which ultimately fuels depression. Social media allows us to compare everything, and we do, such as relationships, diets, figures, hair, clothes, cars, holidays, and lifestyles, not just with our friends, but also with total strangers and celebrities. It seems that even money and sunshine for some, wears off very quickly. However, in today's world, health issues differ from the past, in that health and fitness is contended with physiological issues such as anxiety, loneliness, financial woes and ever-demanding jobs. Are the jobs any more demanding as our jobs were in the sixties, whereby the hours were longer, and working conditions less comfortable, or is it that young people today, are not self-motivated, un-disciplined, complacent, and don't get the job satisfaction that we did?

So, what is a health freak? A health freak is a person who is obsessed about their health, and one day will find themselves lying in hospital, dying of nothing.

For some reason, health freaks tend to believe they are superior to the rest of us, and consider themselves 'cool', with their salads and green teas, in cafés and restaurants, sitting with their comrades, that are still in their gym gear. A false camaraderie of people, who otherwise have nothing in common. Sometimes, they can be, (as they say) naughty, and cheat, by sneaking into Burger King or Baskin Robins, once or twice a week to pig out!

Why suffer, that's what I say. If there is something you like, have it if you can, and, if you feel guilty, just think of the many people that would love to indulge – those with various allergies and diseases, or for other reasons don't have the privilege of eating or drinking what they want, just as we do.

Yes, we know that smoking and too much alcohol is bad for you, and you say dairy products contribute to high cholesterol, really? And, too much fruit is unhealthy, because the liver turns the excess fructose intake into triglycerides that are stored in fat cells throughout the body. Thank you for that information. Did you know that people suffering from hypothyroid should not eat cabbage? You see, cabbage releases goitrogens, a chemical that reacts with iodine. In other words, the iatrogenic substance interferes with iodine uptake in the thyroid. Now, fuck off.

And, what about this generation of the *gym freaks*? Those guys that drive their car the three or four kilometres to the gym, take the lift to the first floor, and start walking on a treadmill, before lifting weights. I would find it most aggravating to work out in a gym, knowing what I know. There always appears to be a couple of big, fat, muscular, arrogant bastards that spend most of their time in the gym, and think they own the place. Between lifting weights, these guys need mirror space, there are a lot of mirrors, as gym freaks need to look at themselves constantly, and focus on their gains. You must be careful not to take up too much of their mirror space. Even in the bathroom, while you are washing your hands, someone will come up behind you, and put their arms around you, to reach for the sink to wash their hands, all the while gazing at themselves intensely in the mirror. There are those that have not learned gym etiquette, trying to make conversation, oblivious to others taking rest periods that want some quiet free time – these types have no sense of body language when one looks at them with an expression suggesting that they should just shut the fuck up. Others have a sweaty aroma that enters the room before they do and it lingers everywhere they go – they forget to wipe the sweat off the bench they have been working out on. Then there are those bastards that hog that particular piece of equipment that you went to the gym for, knowing they are keeping you waiting.

Ladies, if you are thinking of dating a gym guy, there are some things that you really need to understand.

Remember there will always be the three of you, him, the gym and yourself.

He won't take you to visit your favourite restaurants and pig out on those delicious meals you enjoy. Even alcohol is out. The main conversations during mealtimes will be health, fitness and food.

Tank tops, tracksuit, bottoms, a protein shake bottle at hand, will become the normal attire, with endless piles of sweaty gym clothes, waiting to be washed.

Going to bed together after midnight on weekends, laying in late, romantically hugging, before getting up to an unhealthy, but tasty greasy brunch will not happen. Early to bed, and early to rise.

Wall to wall mirrors in the apartment are a must. He must be able to see his body wherever he goes. He will observe his own and gym mates' body more than yours.

His favourite date nights will be working out together and all vacations will involve frequenting the gym.

I often see the muscle guy tourists, while I am out on one of my walks, around the Bangkok area, where I stay, they are normally in pairs, walking slowly, probably on their way to the gym. I enjoy 'people watching' when I go out. I came across two the other day, walking side by side towards me. Both had tank tops and very tight shorts, bursting with muscles. They were carrying bottled water, and had that aggressive, but sad and lonely expression on their faces, as they do. Their arms were pointed outwards, because of the expanded muscles in their arms and shoulders, they couldn't rest them down their sides. I was going to say, "Come on guys, this is Bangkok, why don't you just dump those water bottles, and we will go bar hopping, and drink a few beers around Patpong, and get drunk. We can shoot some pool, then check out the girls in a couple of Go-Go Bars, watch a Ping Pong show, see a Lady boy Cabaret, and eat a Thai curry on the way home, just as it is getting light." I was going to, but one of them just pushed me out the way, as they strolled past.

Chapter 4
The Sixties in Retro

The past is a great place, and I don't want to erase it, or regret it, but I don't want to be its prisoner either.

Mick Jagger.

I am drinking in an Irish pub in Silom Road, Bangkok, and watching The Beatles live. The Thai Beatles Cover Band to be exact. The bar is full to capacity, and the crowd is made up of after work Thai nationals, expat tourists, and back packers of many different nationalities. The Thai Beatles Tribute Band, complete with mop hairstyles and matching Beatle style suits, are blasting out songs, such as '*Hey Jude*', '*Let it Be*', and '*Ob-La-De-Ob-La-Da*'. The crowd are moving and singing along. They know all the words. Elderly couples are dancing, as they did back in their teens (well, trying to). Guys put their beers down and cannot resist playing the air guitar. A guy sitting next to me, at the bar leans over, and reminds me that The Beatles and their songs go back more than fifty years. (I know, I was there all those years ago).

A couple of nights previous, I was in the Muzzic Café, situated along Bangkok's Patpong night market, when the local band performing there, opened their gig with Led Zeppelin's '*Stairway to Heaven*' (A song voted number three in the top 100 of greatest rock songs of all time), followed by Jimi Hendrix hit of 1967, '*Hey Joe*'. The crowd of mixed expats, young and old, were ecstatic. Jimmy Hendrix is, today, still considered by many as the greatest guitarist that ever lived.

What is it that makes the sixties' decade so special, even today? Why does a tiny sixties design Morris Mini Minor car get as much attention, when spotted on the road, as does a Lamborghini or Rolls Royce? And, what about the E-Type Jaguar? When launched in 1961, Enzo Ferrari called it, "*The most beautiful car ever made.*" Is there a commercial aircraft in the world today that has the elegance and glamour, and touches the hearts of the public, as did the supersonic passenger aircraft Concorde, which had a maximum speed over twice the speed of sound? And why were the sixties' generation so different from other generations?

The nineteen sixties was a decade of rapid change, with many defining aspects, such as music, fashion, and technology, where young people were finally given a voice and freedom to do and say what they wanted. That's not exactly true! They were not given a voice, they decided that it was time the younger, working class had a voice, and that they would make their own choices, and not be dictated to by the upper classes of that era. The old establishment wanted to continue as before, whereas the younger generation, who were better educated and informed, wanted change. The swinging sixties has been named as the most defining decade of the 20th century. From protest and war, to the space race, The Beatles, innovative technologies, fashion and politics. The events of that tumultuous ten-year period transformed the world, making it the most transformative decade of the modern era.

I grew up in the then-industrial city of Coventry, which at the time, was in the process of rebuilding after the war, whereby three-quarters of the city's factories were destroyed, and as many as 4,500 homes were lost in one night. Coventry was the heart of British industry at that time. It was the night of 14th November 1940, when Hitler sent over 500 bombers, and dropped as many as 500 tons of high explosives, 30,000 incendiaries and landmines over eleven continuous hours. By August 1942, the city had suffered almost forty similar attacks.

We were post-war kids, with no first-hand experience of the war, but the consequences were still evident through our parents, a generation that had given their youth to the war effort, many never to get over the trauma, whilst others worked diligently to rebuild their lives.

My earliest recollections as a young boy, are going with my father, at that time a lorry driver (sometime during the mid-1950s), to deliver wood from a timber yard to Coventry, at an area, which appeared to be an enormous building site, as far as the eye could see, in every direction. I remember an aunt we would visit in Coventry, who still had an air raid shelter in her back garden, and a neighbour that suffered from shell shock (known today as post-traumatic stress). Many soldiers were afflicted, as a result of the war.

I still remember, as a young boy, the unshaven, unkempt 'tramps', in their trench coats, passing through the village where we lived, before we moved to the city. They would knock on our door, looking for a hot drink and some food to help them on their way. My father would take them in and give them what he could.

It was only years later that I came to understand, that these were not tramps at all. They were men who during their youth, had volunteered to do their bit, and serve the nation for six years of war. Once the war was over and they had served their purpose, they had been discarded and abandoned. They spent their days, unable to fit back into society, running from nightmares, and looking for friends and family that were never found.

It is said that Coventry was a national centre of urban regeneration, economic growth and social change after the Second World War. Although not appreciated at the time, I now know that growing up in Coventry during the boom years of the sixties was a unique experience, and how lucky I was. My friends and workmates were from Scottish, Irish, Welsh and Northern families, whose parents had come looking for employment after the war, to rebuild Coventry, and to work in its factories. Suddenly, simple working-class people had full-time employment, could afford to buy cars, and own their own homes. We worked in the many factories that built cars, aircraft engines, tractors, and machines, learning trades and skills that in later years, when the industries declined, workers from Coventry took with them, to all corners of the world.

The guys I associated with at that time were proud to be factory workers, bricklayers, carpenters – you name it. I was happy clocking in and out of the factory every day, stinking of machine oil, sneaking into the toilets to look at pornographic magazines, smoking Wills Woodbine cigarettes, drinking pints of Brew XI Bitter (beer), hanging out in the working man's club, playing dominoes, darts and snooker, and happier still to receive a wage packet at the end of the week. I was sixteen years of age but could have been twenty-six. I suppose a kid of that age today would be on his skateboard, playing computer games, reading Harry Potter books or possibly taking drugs. In any event, we would have one thing in common, in that, the word retirement, would not have entered our vocabulary.

Chapter 5
Dubai to Bangkok

It is not the strongest of the species that survive, nor the most intelligent, but the one most responsive to change.

Charles Darwin.

I have lived and worked in the United Arab Emirates for thirty years. Dubai continues to develop, and today is one of the most modern cities in the world. It has become a destination for tourists that mixes modern culture with history. It has world-class shopping, entertainment, sports, and adventure, and has become a major business hub in the Middle East for the oil & gas industries, commodity trading, and banking. I believe I have been a good citizen in all those years and have contributed in my part to its success. I have brought up three children (one of which was born there), who all went through the local schooling system, settled, and are today living and working in Dubai. The only crimes I committed in all that time, was one each speeding and parking fines.

What one learns with living in Dubai, after some time, is that a person is only as good as what they have to offer. Dubai has developed a lifestyle where one's hard-earned salary is absorbed right back into the system. The days of making and saving money, for the majority, have passed. I know of many people, coming to Dubai, and getting sucked into the Dubai lifestyle, living far above their means, sadly leaving in debt, with nothing to show for it. I found that, when I retired from my work, and my resident/employment visa was cancelled, I immediately became an alien in the country, and was sometimes treated like one, when trying to do the day-to-day things where a visa or ID is required. So, when I passed the airport immigration one day, and the immigration officer eyed me up and down, before stamping my passport with a thirty-day visit visa, and said in a not particularly friendly way, "So how long do you intend to stay here?" I realised that Dubai can no longer be my home.

So, why Bangkok? Well, as I mentioned, the lifestyle is affordable, and it is rich in culture and traditions, it has an atmosphere like no other city, but it is much more than that, it is charming and exotic. Having visited Bangkok over the years. and done or visited most of the recommended tourist attractions, which no longer appeal to me, I thought I was getting to know, and understand Bangkok, until now, I realise that I haven't touched the surface. Yes, it's easy to criticise Bangkok, for example, it is stifling hot most of the time, crowded and polluted, rumour is that it is sinking a few inches every year, but don't ask me about other places I have visited, unless you want to hear some negative remarks and comments.

Then, what is the attraction, and why would a retired sixty ex-British mod want to pass his days here?

The truth is, day-to-day life on the streets of Bangkok is bad organisation, very well organised. It is a city of contradictions. Thailand, does, of course, have laws for the environment, and everything else, but most rules can be ignored or interpreted to suit. There is little bureaucracy. People are generally friendly and calm. It is strategically placed, surrounded by many interesting countries worth visiting, such as Vietnam, Myanmar, Cambodia and Malaysia, plus places like Bali, Singapore and Hong Kong can be reached in around three hours. The traffic can be horrendous, but one can take a *tuk-tuk* or a breathtakingly, exciting ride on the back of a motorcycle taxi, for just a few Bhat, and weave in and out of the vehicles, along sidewalks, busy with pedestrians, take the sky train and get a bird's eye view of the city, sit back and relax in a candy-coloured taxi, which are not so expensive, ride the water taxi along the Chao Phraya River, or a boat along the canals. In public places, at 08.00 and 18.00 every day, and in cinemas before a movie, the national anthem is played. Locals and others stop. and stand still. Not to do so is lack of respect (and illegal). How nice it would be if people respected my country's national anthem in such a manner.

Thailand has experienced more military coups than any other country. Since 1932 (when the absolute monarchy was replaced by a constitutional monarchy), there has been an astonishing twelve successful attempts, as well as seven unsuccessful, thirty governments and eighteen constitutions.

It is said, "When we first see a country, we don't see things as they are, we see them as we are!"

I feel now, and only after spending time and exploring Bangkok, I am beginning, only beginning, to see things how they are. So many things fascinate me. Where else would one find a young female golf caddie with a name like 'Superporn', who massages your neck and shoulders, and cools you with her fan, whilst waiting on the tee box for the group ahead to move on? And young ladies, with interesting names, such as Tin, Pin, Duck or Fiat. The young lady, who kneels in front of a Shrine, in the main street, of the Hindu God Ganesh, and prays for good karma, wealth, and wisdom, before going into Nana Plaza, where she works in a go-go bar, dances naked, and sells herself to customers. Gilded gold spires and pagodas soaring above, and in between the modern buildings. Eating in the street, sitting on a small stool, sharing a plastic table with persons of different classes, such as executives, office workers, street salesmen, back packers, and those down on their luck. We stick chilies, fish sauce and bean sprouts (from grubby plastic containers) into our bowls of chicken, pork, or shrimp noodles, and slurp away. Would tourists, that think this is a novelty, really sit in a street with the traffic exhaust pollution, the roar of tuk-tuks and motorcycles in their ears, garbage below their feet and toilet rolls as paper napkins, do this anywhere else in the world?

One walks along the side of the road, avoiding the traffic, because a street market has set up on the pavement, selling clothes, fruit and fire grilled meats on a barbeque stand, which was not there yesterday, and popped up out of nowhere.

Jumping out of the way of motorcycle taxis and delivery boys, who veer off the road, onto the sidewalk, so as to pass the lines of slow-moving traffic. I know Bangkok has taught me patience, when I smile as they go by, and they respond with a nod. That doesn't happen in most other countries, and if it did, they would probably get punched on the nose by some angry pedestrian. It's interesting to note, that for some reason, pedestrian crossings in Bangkok are reported to be the most dangerous places to cross the road. It was reported recently that authorities were considering doing away with them. A motorist later commented "I wondered what those stripes on the road were for anyway". Strangely, in spite of its traffic congestion, and unlike other big cities, there is a notable lack of car horns being sounded in the streets.

Recently, there was panic all over the city, when the headline of the daily newspaper, the Bangkok Post, read, "*Anger in Bangkok as city bans street food*," – it went on to say, "All street food will be banned from all Bangkok main roads, under a clean-up campaign." A local government official went on to say, "This has prompted outcry and anguish around our city, which is obsessed with food and famed for its spicy roadside cuisine." Chief adviser to Bangkok's Governor said that about two-thirds of the city's 30,000 street stalls of all kinds will be removed for hygiene reasons, and to leave space for pedestrians. A spokesman for a Bangkok tour agency said that to clean out the venders, is as if you are cleaning out our culture itself, you meet the people who cook, you can interact with them, and you can see what the ingredients are. Many Bangkok residents believe that this organised chaos is part of the city's charm, and provides an affordable food option for all, over the city, at a time when the cost of living is surging. For 10 baht (£0.23), you can still buy a stick of grilled meat, and for 35 baht (£0.80) a bowl of chicken noodles. Critics say that it is an attempt by the current government to remodel Bangkok around Singapore, by enforcing regulations that have, for a long time, been abandoned or ignored. Only in Bangkok, would the people quietly hope that a beautification campaign falls flat.

“Don’t they sell tires?” was the reaction of one seventy-two-year-old lady, who had just been told that she had been awarded a Michelin Star for her outstanding street food. She admitted that she had never heard of the Michelin Star. Whilst the award boosted her sales, it became a disruption to her already busy lifestyle, when tourists that had heard about her cuisine, began queuing to sample her food, and the many more that came just to take photographs.

I am intrigued as to why Thais can eat four or five times a day, and not get fat, and how they walk in the sweltering heat, and don’t sweat like us Europeans. They say we smell like butter. I see a family pass by on a small motorcycle, dad, with a young child in front of him, and wife sitting behind with baby in her arms, none wearing a protective helmet, another with a pet dog between himself and the handlebars, the dog wearing sunglasses. Who cannot love this place? Thais love and feed scabby stray dogs that roam the streets. It is said to be unlucky to have your haircut on a Wednesday. Many salons still observe this superstition by scheduling their weekly day off on a Wednesday.

I am also intrigued with the Thai’s love and fear of invisible spirits known as *phi* that they believe live amongst them. To keep the *phi* happy, they put up shrines everywhere. You will find them in the streets, in restaurants and homes, in front of shops and banks, even inside taxis. If they cut down a tree, or build on some land, they will build a shrine for the tree or earth *phi* to apologise for the disturbance caused. You will see shrines, surrounded with offerings such as jasmine, little wooden elephants, plastic dolls, sweets and soft drinks, even the odd bottle of beer. You may, or may not, be interested to know, that only foreigners refer the capital as Bangkok. In Thai, it is often called *Krung Thep Maka Nakhon*, or just *Krung Thep*. However, the full name is something like, ‘*Krung Thep Mahanakhon Amon Rattanakosin Mahinthara Ayutthaya Mahadilok Phop Noppharat Ratchathani Burirom Udomratchaniwet Mahasathan Amon Piman Awatan Sathit Sakkathattiya*

Witsanukam'. Certified as the longest place name in the world in the Guinness book of records.

The official translation reads – *the great city of angels, the supreme unconquerable land of the great immortal divinity (Indra), the royal capital of nine noble gems, the pleasant city with plenty of grand royal palaces, and divine paradises for the reincarnated deity.*

So, what attracts me to this place? In my subconscious mind, am I in some way re-living or learning from the new sights, sounds and experiences, just as I did as a young man, growing up during the sixties?

Today, young people learn and see so much on social media, and therefore, never have the feeling of discovering by experiencing the many things that life has to offer for themselves, they know everything, but have actually experienced very little. You see them in groups, in shopping malls and cafés, heads down, absorbed in their mobile phones and appliances. Are these kids truly free, if they cannot spend a full day without the apps on their smart phone? When we were young, we would spend hours with friends, debating, arguing questioning, such things as sport, music, movies and, of course, the opposite sex.

My first job (until I got run over by a mechanic, testing the breaks on a car, which didn't work) was in a car repair garage. On my first day, I was put to work with an Indian mechanic by the name of Moony Lal. During one conversation, he told me he had two wives, an old one for her loyalty, and a young one for the fucking. I was fourteen years of age! What do you tell your mum when she welcomes you home from work, and asks what did you learn at work today? On my first day in the car factory, still fourteen, whilst being shown around the workshops by an elder apprentice, I was introduced to a fatherly looking gentleman. He smiled, shook my hand, and whilst welcoming me to my new assignment, to the amusement of all those around, firmly grabbed my testicles with his other hand. The guy would probably be locked up in today's world, and be the excuse for my later misadventures, experimenting with drink and drugs.

Walking the streets of Bangkok, taking in the many different sounds, smells of street food being prepared, and the unusual sights, some pleasant and some not so pleasant, takes me back to when the travelling Fun Fair would visit our city, in the early sixties. Every year, they would set up on Hearsall Common, not far from our home. Even if we didn't have a much money in our pockets, it was interesting to wander around, and watch all the fun of the Fair.

The excitement started before arriving at the fairground, when one could hear the music and see the lights of the rides in the distance, and families, old and young, hurrying to get there. I was a 'people watcher' at a very young age, as I remember being intrigued by those who worked in the fairgrounds. The fairground workers looked simple but tough, with dark complexions, such as gypsies, others had the appearance of '*Teddy Boys*' from the fifties' decade, with their iconic hairstyles, drainpipe trousers and thick sole suede loafers. What young kid did not want to work on the dodgems, hanging on the back of a dodgem car, impressing a couple of good-looking screaming girls, by showing them how to steer through crazy dodgem traffic, coming from all directions?

Wandering around the fairground, one would come across things that we were not accustomed to seeing at that time, such as coconuts, gold fish, tortoises, and the wonderful aromas of toffee apples, candyfloss, and how the hot dogs smelled and tasted far better then, than they do today! I also remember the humming sounds, and smell of diesel from the generators, and the ozone (which some describe as smelling like sparks!) from the electrical-driven dodgem cars and rides. There were the terrified screams of those riding the waltzers or the octopus, to the sound of music such as '*Rocking Goose*', blasting in the background. I seem to recall that there were steam organs at that time.

I would stand and watch those trying their luck on the sideshows, such as the coconut shy. They would throw a small wooden ball at coconuts, sitting on stands, and try, and knock them off, to win a prize. The coconuts were suspiciously fixed very firm to the stands. The satisfaction of knocking a coconut off its stand had far more value than the cheap plastic prizes that were there to win. Occasionally, you would see a lucky winner, strolling around with a premium prize of a goldfish in a plastic bag.

Just as today, my curiosity then, always got the better of me, and I would waste the little money I had, that would have been far better spent on the rides. I just could not resist going into the tacky sideshows that invited one to see weird exhibits of freaks, such as the Bearded or Tattooed Lady, Siamese Twins, Tom Thumb or the Leprechaun. I think it cost about sixpence. I would come out, completely confused and disappointed, after seeing worn-out old photographs of ladies with beards and tattoos, and unusual characters who were obviously long-deceased.

The Ghost Train was popular. The carriage would wind its way through dark tunnels, with the effigies of ghosts, and terrifying screams, there was the sound of thunder, the lightning would show just enough light to see Dracula-like figures, homing in on the carriage, large black crows hovering overhead, and human-like skeletons, laying on the ground. It would take you through dark caves, with cobwebs brushing the face, and bats fluttering around, their eyes bright against the darkness.

I visited a fair ground some years later, with a couple of friends, after we had been in a pub, and were far worse the ware from drink. One of them, who was probably a little old, and a little drunk for it, despite our protests, decided he wanted to go for a ride on a ghost train, for old times' sake. I got a feeling that something was going to happen. Well, he decided to jump out halfway round, and play at being a ghost. He started pulling peoples ears and hair, and screaming at them, as they went past. Grown adults were coming out of the tunnel, and getting off the ride, terrified. My friend was fine, until he tried to get a ride out, and found that on the back of the cars, there was nowhere to stand or hold onto. He reappeared, coming out of the tunnel, hanging around a guy's throat, who was panic-stricken and screaming his head off.

The guy’s young son, sitting next to him, was looking bored, and wondering what all the fuss was about.

Chapter 6
The Mods

One of the great things about the British Mod movement was that being macho was no longer the only measure of manhood.

Pete Townshend.

As my American friend may have inadvertently pointed out, becoming a mod was a lifestyle choice that people still carry with them today. Mods should not be compared with other cultural fads, such as Teddy Boys, Skin Heads and Punk Rockers, all of which have come and gone. Mods were mainly working-class teenagers. The economy was booming, and many of these youngsters had little responsibility, but had money in their pockets. They saw little value in saving for the future and lived for the moment.

By 1965, mods had their own monthly magazines, '*The Mod*', and '*The Mods*', and their own television programme. Friday evenings were dominated by one programme, which proved to be the best pop show ever, *'Ready Steady Go',* which was first broadcast in 1963, and promised, *"The weekend starts here",* and it did. The excitement of waiting all week to watch our favourite performers was over, the show featured bands, such as the Rolling Stones, The Who, The Small Faces and the Kinks, all who had adopted the mod style. Jimi Hendrix made his first television appearance in Britain on Ready Steady Go with 'Hey Joe', after which, his club tour sold out, and he was added to a nationwide tour with other well-known artists. We also got our first chance to watch live on TV, American Soul, and R&B artists such as, The

Temptations, Aretha Franklin, James Brown, Ike, and Tina Turner, or Percy Sledge.

From the opening title music, the Surfaris' '*Wipe Out*', and later Manfred Mann's '*5-4-3-2-1*', the show was full of activity and a unique atmosphere, with off-the-cuff interviews, with the artists and band members between performances. The general public were allowed to hang out or dance on the studio floor and mingle with the celebrities. The show, for a while, was presented by Dusty Springfield, but the best-known presenter would be Cathy McGowan, a typical teenager of the day that answered an advertisement who, from one day to the next, found herself as a presenter introducing, and interviewing the stars. Her inexperience, innocence, and stumbling over her lines, made her more than less popular with the audiences. She became the face of Ready Steady Go, and her casual dress and style got her the name of Queen of the Mods.

1964 was probably the first year in which the mods came to public attention outside of London, when they clashed with rival youth group, the '*Rockers*'. Rockers preferred a classic style of leather jackets, tight jeans, pointed-toe shoes, traditional Teddy Boy hairstyles, rock n roll, and powerful motorbikes. They were often gang members or groups, sporting the name of the gang they belonged to, stencilled to the back of their leather jackets. Influenced, I assume, by Americas Hell's Angels. The mods, in turn, sported short, well-kept hair, smart, continental clothes, Italian Vespa and Lambretta motor scooters, and music, by newly formed mod-style bands.

The disturbances began at the coastal town of Clacton, and spread to Brighton, Margate Bournemouth, and Hastings, during the Bank Holiday weekends in that year. The headlines read '*Bank Holiday Mayhem*', '*Clacton Torn Apart over Easter Weekend*'. There appeared to be no particular animosity between the two groups, and when a Bank Holiday came along, like any typical family, they also followed the great British tradition of heading to the seaside. Where they went, often depended on where they came from. There were no particular battle plans involved. Although, in many places, it was a non-event, as far as the police were concerned, the media however were all over it. Television news flashes such as, *"Todays bank holiday began with tourists flocking to the coast but ended up with them fleeing for their lives as Mods and Rockers turned beaches into battlefields."* (I am smiling). *"Terror on the beaches, families were trapped in a shocking showdown, which sparked moral panic about the state of British youth today."* And what about, *"Civilization, as we know it, has ended."* We were proud to see a Coventry kid's photo appear on the front of a daily newspaper, standing on a beach wall in Brighton, wrapping a deck chair over a rocker's head. What did become evident, was the fact, some of these kids had money, when, one of them, after appearing in court, and was given a hefty fine, simply took a cheque book out of his pocket, and wrote out a cheque. There were no credit cards at that time.

My first recollection of mods would be around that time, when a couple of my elder brother's friends would visit our house. They had short, smart haircuts, soft, round-toe shoes, and loose-fitting casual trousers, and I was impressed as to how cool they acted. Their appearance was a complete contrast to how they had looked, when I last met them, a few months earlier. I had just started work, was earning a weekly wage, and started noticing the new fashions that were appearing in magazines, and the styles my favourite bands were sporting.

On reflection, I suppose turning mod at that time was not unlike coming out of the closet and admitting that you were gay (especially in an industrial city like Coventry). My crowd, of young construction or factory workers, like myself, would meet most evenings at the entrance to the local park, and just hang around, kick a ball about, or get up to mischief. I remember the first time, approaching them, wearing a pair of Levi's (I suppose they were boot-cut, uncommon at that time), Hush Puppies shoes, a polo shirt, and a tweed jacket, with flaps on the pockets, and a fresh haircut.

There was a crowd of them, standing around, some sitting on the park gate, and I heard someone say out loud, "Fucking hell, Mart's turned mod," followed by complete silence, as they watched me walk towards them. There was silence for some time, as they looked me up and down until the banter, which I had expected started.

"He looks like a fucking twat."

"Tell me who cut your hair like that, and I will get him for you."

"He must have stolen that jacket from his grandad."

My friends were not particularly Rockers, but their styles leaned that way, however, as time passed, they saw for themselves that times were changing. Often, one would admire my shirt or shoes, and quietly ask me where I bought them, others would appear with haircuts that looked suspiciously casual.

By 1966, I had made a lot of new friends from working in the factory, most of them were a couple of years older than me, which made me feel good. During the week, we would hang around the factory, working man's club, and at weekends, we would hit the pubs around the city centre. The mod culture was in its prime, at that time, and gangs from all over the city would crowd the pubs, moving from one to another. We would move between pubs, such as the Market Tavern, The City Arms, The Coventry Climax, and The Jaguar, which were, at that time, always crowded and rowdy. The jukeboxes would be blasting out music by The Beatles, Percy Sledge, The Beach Boys and the Supremes. Some guys would be high on amphetamine, known as purple hearts, or dextrin, which would sell in little packets of eight pills for £1.00. We all knew who the pushers (as they were called) were, who would wander between the pubs, making deals. They were stupid enough to act, and look like drug dealers, thinking it was cool, with collars turned up, and wearing sunglasses. Marijuana, or hashish, was also available, which for some reason was called 'shit'. We all tried that stuff, but only to be part of the in-crowd. The pills just kept you awake, if you were going to an all-night party, and you would irritate others, by babbling on like an idiot about nothing, which was known as verbling! We were in a club, one night, and one of our crowd, an Irish lad, managed to get a dance with a girl. Trying to impress her, and acting cool, the conversation went,

"Hi, how you doing?"

"I am ok."

"Do you want some shit?"

"I am sorry, what did you say?"

"I asked you if you want some shit."

Followed by him receiving a generous slap around the face, and the girl storming off the dance floor to re-join her friends. We can only assume that she was not into the drug scene, and over the sound of the Rolling Stones '*I Can't Get No Satisfaction*', she thought he was asking her if she wanted to go to the toilet.

Our group was not particularly impressed with the drugs scene, we were factory workers with a pub culture. Beer was our thing. For some reason, we would judge people by how much booze they could consume, which somehow might have come from the Irish influence amongst us. Comments would be made like, "Patrick's a great guy, you should see how many pints of Guinness he can put away." On the other hand, they might talk about someone and say, "He's okay I suppose, but he doesn't drink fuck all!"

It is so sad to visit Coventry these days, and see the pub culture declining, and the numbers of pubs that are closing their doors. At that time, Coventry had around 250 pubs, many with unusual names, such as The Bug and Black Cat, The Bricklayers' Arms, The Rose and Woodbine, The Elephant and Castle, The Dun Cow, and who could walk past the Jolly Collier, without stopping by for a pint. Some nights, I would walk along Spon End, an area close to the newly reconstructed city centre, very much a contrast with very old buildings, some from Tudor Times. I'd stop off in the Black Horse, and sit amongst the Irish workers, who had finished their shift in the Renold Chain factory next door and had come in for a few pints and some craic. I would pop in the Old Windmill for a game of dominoes, a very old 15th century building, divided into small rooms with low ceilings, fireplaces, and uneven floors. The pubs were all very different, with their decors, atmospheres, and the type of cliental or locals, normally from around the neighbourhood, where they were situated.

There were considerable differences between the Mods at that time, which could be divided into three groups, being the Mainstream mods, the Scooter Boys and the Hardline mods.

The mainstream mods were from the London areas, and could be described as 'dedicated followers of fashion'. They came from wealthy families, had good jobs, and were always up to date with the latest fashions. They wore Italian suits, shopped at the most expensive boutiques in Carnaby Street, Oxford Street and Chelsea's Kings Road. They gathered in café's and fashionable pubs and restaurants.

The Scooter Boys were more casual, with ex-US surplus army parkas, woollen or cashmere sweaters, Levi jeans and desert boots, suitable attire for hanging around on their scooters, which they fitted over the front, a mass of highly chromed headlights, fog lamps, antennas and wing mirrors, attached to the handlebars.

Hardline mods were generally from the cities north of London, lower-paid, young industrial, and blue-collar workers, such as ourselves. We couldn't afford scooters (maybe, could have if we hadn't drunk and smoked so much). How we envied those guys, when they cruised by on their flashy machines with a mod girl, sitting behind them, with their arms around their waists. I suppose they were good guys, but they didn't drink fuck all. Our fashions were not as flamboyant as the mainstream, but smarter than the scooter boys.

The mod culture was more than just the clothes, it was a way of life. Everything we did had some reason and thought behind it. We had to be cool at all times. The type of clothes we wore, the music we listened to, and the crowd we hung around with, the bars and clubs we frequented, were all a reflection of ourselves. Even the cigarettes we smoked were to impress.

Cigarettes were part of the background to everyday life in the mid-sixties, in fact, doctors were known to tell their patients that a cigarette was a good way to relax and release stress. Most men and women lit up, and even school kids took up smoking. Although, most people had no idea of the health risks. Wills Woodbine and Park Drive were cheap unfiltered, and the working man's favourites but became to be seen as an old man's product, and so new brands were launched to satisfy the new trends and modern classes. To show some culture, we changed to Embassy Filter Tipped, which were launched for younger people, and took the market by storm, a smaller brand, such as Players No 6 were popular with the women. (How many of my mother's Players No 6 did I secretly help myself to, to smoke on the way to school?) Then, there were king sized sophisticated brands, such as Peter Stuyvesant and Pall Mall that were way above our class.

The cigarette adverts we grew up with, gave the impression that it was healthy to smoke, and the brand you chose was a status symbol. Such advertising was commonplace, and often featured happy, healthy-looking people, some leading sports figures, and others well-known entertainers. Indeed, with the added approval from top movie stars, smoking's image was both cool and glamorous. The adverts were designed to make smoking feel irresistible.

An earlier TV advert for Camel Cigarettes ran with the slogan, 'More Doctors Smoke Camels than any other cigarette'. In a recent survey, doctors in all branches of medicine were asked what cigarettes they smoke. And, the brand name most did was '*Camel*'. The footage went on to show a doctor, sitting at his desk, puffing away at a cigarette, whilst his assistant nurse is standing over him, reviewing a medical report.

Menthol-flavoured cigarettes tried to catch the market. Salam cigarettes sounded irresistible, the packet showing a good-looking couple walking romantically together in the countryside, with a caption below that read 'The flavour that's spring time fresh, refreshes your taste, Salam, the menthol flavour and rich tobacco taste'. There were more macho brands, such as Marlboro, which sported on the cover, a rugged, good-looking, rural, cowboy guy, with a caption, 'Come to where the flavour is, come to Marlboro country', although rumours were that the Marlboro man eventually died of lung cancer. Well, what did he expect? His contract apparently stated he must smoke as many as forty Marlboro cigarettes a day. Many other brands hit the market such as Kensitas, Bristol and Strand, all of which were considered very unfashionable and suitable, only for loners, and finally flopped. There was one popular TV advert, showing a man in different awkward situations, and looking very perturbed, when to the sound in the background of classical music, and the words, '*Happiness is a Cigar Called Hamlet*'. He lights up a small cigar, inhales, and breaks into a satisfied smile as he exhales the smoke.

It was not unusual to see celebrities and sportsmen light up a cigarette, whilst appearing on TV talk shows, or when they were being interviewed. I remember watching an interview with Mick Jagger one evening. He kept lighting up from a pack of Benson & Hedges Pure Gold that were on the table in front of him. The Benson & Hedges *'Pure Gold'* campaign had a slightly tongue-in-cheek take on the value of gold. "*What do you keep in reserve for special occasions?*" Answer: "*Pure Gold from Benson and Hedges*." They came in a pure gold colour, flip-top packet, and cost more than we could afford. Sure enough, however, the next night, when we met in the bar, a couple of the guys were sitting shamelessly, smoking Benson & Hedges, with the packets laying on the table for all to see. They had obviously seen the Jagger interview the night before.

Being a mod was about creating one's own style, we were, of course, influenced by the bands, and what they were wearing on Ready Steady Go on a Friday night, and first thing Saturday go down the town centre to look for the same or something similar. But, a piece of clothing designed and purchased from a boutique in Kings Road was hardly going to show up in Coventry. The only place I could find Levi Jeans was a stall in Coventry Market, they cost around five pounds sterling, which was not cheap, compared to other brands. They would shrink in the wash, so we had to buy the next size up. Then, there was the job of giving them the well-worn look.

Today, looking back, I feel sympathy for my poor parents, who really believed that we should have been satisfied with everything we had at that time, they could not understand why young people wanted to be rebels, and had to challenge the establishment, and change everything that they thought we should be content with. Today, I can only smile and be grateful when I think of the understanding and patience, they had with me, growing up. I remember my dad looking out of the window and watching me on my hands and knees in the back garden, scrubbing my jeans on the paving. The conversation went something like this.

"What are you doing?"

"I'm scrubbing my jeans."

"Why are you scrubbing your jeans, they are new you just bought them."

"Yeah, but I want them to look old and well-worn."

Silence, and confused thought for a minute, then shouts to my mum.

"Vera, I think your son needs his head examined!"

"Why is that, my dear?"

"You know those brand-new jeans he just bought? Well, he's in the garden scrubbing them, he wants them to look old."

"Don't worry dear, you know what these kids are like, sit down, I will bring your dinner in."

We had to be casual. The way we walked, the way we talked, and the way we looked, even having a hair cut in the early days, when the shorter style was fashionable, we would tell the barber to leave the back natural, leaving the pencil in (the pencil being that pointed bit of hair at the back of the neck), a square neck was definitely out, and so was a 'DA', the rockers choice, otherwise known as a ducks-arse. I remember when the first ten-pin bowling alley opened in Coventry, it was very American, and a cool place to hang out in, and be seen. Some of the lads took a liking to the casual-looking bowling shoes that were provided, in return for leaving your own shoes, when you bowled. So, the thing to do, was to go bowling, with a very old pair of shoes that you didn't want anymore, keep the bowling shoes when you finished your game, and leave your old ones behind.

Desert Boots were popular with jeans. They were deemed the world's first '*dress casual shoe*'. The story is, that Nathan Clark, a British army officer stationed in Burma, noticed many of his officers wearing simple suede boots with crepe soles when they were off-duty. They were comfortable, and perfect for the terrain. He learned that they originated from a bazaar in Cairo. He made cut-out patterns and drawings of them, and sent them home to his village in Somerset, believing they could be a signature model for his family business. The response from the directors was that they would never sell, so on his return, Nathan travelled to America to show his Desert Boot at the Chicago Shoe Fair in 1949, which was a great success, and so, a global icon was launched. Desert Boots of various styles are still popular today.

The American brand '*Hush Puppies*', made of pigskin with a rubber sole, were also very popular with the mod culture, because of their casual look and comfort. Where did the name Hush Puppies come from? Well, the story goes that the sales manager went on a sales trip to the Southern States. After eating a dinner with a customer, served with a tasty side dish of fried balls of cornmeal batter, which he enjoyed, his customer explained that they were called Hush Puppies, and that the name was developed by the local farmers, who would give the fried dough to their dogs to quiet them down when they were barking or became excited. The salesman thought that it would be a marvellous name for his shoes, and today the Hush Puppies brand, and its dog logo is highly recognised all over the world.

During the mid-sixties, suits, shirts with attachable collars, slim ties and brogues were the attire around the city centre on Friday and Saturday nights. A few of us would meet in The Market Tavern Pub, on Saturday lunchtime for a few beers. We would sit around, telling stupid jokes, insulting each other, arguing football, and brag about the women we had met, or been with the night before. We all thought we were God's gift to women, though most of the stories were fabricated, as we did not have much luck with the women at all. It seems that the free love everyone was talking about during the sixties, didn't find its way to Coventry. The lunchtime drinking sessions were followed by a weekly ritual to visit the various tailor shops around the city centre, and check out the fabrics, go for a fitting, get measured for a new suit, or pay off an instalment. I remember a couple of tailor shops by the names of Burtons and Colliers. Suits cost between twenty pounds sterling, and I was earning around seven pounds a week. Off-the-peg stuff was not an option. I can recall buying my first suit, a steel grey cashmere wool fabric. Even today, I remember that I ordered the trouser legs to have 16-inch knee and 16-inch bottoms. The jacket had slanting pockets, and a ticket pocket, with 2-inch flaps, three buttons, and a single 12-inch vent at the back. All stitching with raised seams. I was around seventeen years of age at that time.

Tailor shops back then, were a little old-fashioned, and catered mainly for the upper class and the elderly. Many tailors found it difficult to come to terms with young working-class guys telling them how they wanted a suit made, and that we didn't want suits cut to their recommendations, double breasted, with wide lapels, buttonholes and trousers with turn-ups. I believe; however, others enjoyed this new trend of turning our backs on tradition, and the challenge of producing suits with modern and continental designs.

Those tailors, despite the custom we gave them, must have secretly dreaded those Saturday afternoons, when half a dozen rowdy drunken young mods would wander into their shop. We would spend hours, having them pull the rolls of cloth from the shelves, and compare, and argue amongst ourselves which designs, and types of materials would be the most fashionable, and the one getting measured for a suit keep changing his mind. I recall my Irish friend, who went for a fitting. He appeared from the changing room, to the amusement of the other customers in the shop, wearing just the jacket, underpants, and socks. The young gay tailor was panicking, and ushering him back to the changing room, with my friend resisting, trying to explain that the trousers are ok, it was just the jacket that needed adjusting. The same guy, when we went into a shoe shop to try on shoes, would explain to the assistant that he needed to see what the shoes were like for dancing. To our horror, he would stand in front of the mirror, doing various unconventional dance steps that resembled a cross between Chubby Checker's twist and the chicken dance. However, when we went to a nightclub, I never saw him dance, as his favourite spot was close to the bar.

Chapter 7
That Retro Feeling

The only reason time seems to be moving rather fast is that sometimes we are too busy living in the past.

Unknown.

The distance between Bangkok and London is 5,800 miles, whereby, France is around 22 miles. For me, it might, just as well, be the other way around.

The lifestyle of the younger Thai generation around Bangkok reminds me so much of my generation. I watch them coming and going, between their work in the exclusive company offices, banks, and buildings, around the Silom, Sathorn, and downtown areas, they frequent the many coffee shops and chic restaurants. As I travel amongst them on the Sky Train, I see a teenage girl with yellow suede boots, green socks, a short skirt above the knee, a long shirt and small trendy backpack, her male friend in yellow shorts and sandals, a printed t-shirt that says '*Let's Get Lost*', on the front, sunglasses, a baseball cap, and leather shoulder bag. They look great together. There is the obvious culture gap between them, and the older generation, who don't let go of the customs, ethnic beliefs, and the culture they have become accustomed to easily. The young ladies, with their fashionable hats, shoes, handbags, sunglasses, and short skirts, and bright lipstick, strolling along the Silom Road, or around the exclusive shopping malls is a fashion show in itself, and a replica of the mod girls, walking along Oxford or Carnaby Streets during the sixties. There is an individualism about the younger generation, they are slightly rebellious, but respectful, as Buddhists are, together with being very fashion-conscious and stylish. Although, walking in Bangkok has become a challenge, due to the obsession of this generation, who are preoccupied with their cell-phones, and them bumping in to you, and each other, not to mention those that keep pausing to take '*selfies*' for no apparent reason, or stopping to take pics of things that appear to be of no interest at all. Backpacks in crowded places really aggravate me.

Thai fashion is becoming a worldwide sensation. In recent years, celebrities from Michelle Obama, Katy Perry, and Jennifer Lopez have flown the flag for Bangkok's designers. The dress that Amy Whitehouse was wearing, on her *Back to Black* album, was a Thai *Disaya* design. Most of the top Thai fashion designers, such as Greyhound, Mob F, Kloset and Sretsis (sisters spelt backwards as it is owned by three sisters), can be found in the exclusive central shopping malls, such as Siam Paragon, Grayson, Emporium, and Central World.

Young Thai bands are very much into western music, old and new. Not yet as good or exciting as the Filipino bands, but they try hard. I sometimes visit O'Mally's, a pub situated below ground level, along Silom Road, where young, local Thais meet for a drink, and congregate after work, before going home. There is normally a jam session or a couple of singers performing, during the evenings. One trio I watched there recently, two young guys and a girl, were singing and playing modern songs and music, but with the '*Skiffle*' sound and tempo. I had completely forgotten about Skiffle and had not heard the sound for many years. It became popular, around the UK, during the late-fifties, early-sixties. The music they made was intriguing, and they were visually entertaining. They were dressed in white shirts, black trousers, bootlace ties, bowler hats, and black swede creepers (round-toed shoes, with very thick soles, adopted by Teddy Boys, during the fifties). They performed with so much enthusiasm and joy, I don't think they would have cared or noticed if the bar was empty. Skiffle music was originally a mixture of jazz, country and blues music, played on simple or improvised instruments, such as a guitar, harmonica, kazoo, washboard, cigar box fiddle, banjo, and musical saw, which originated by improvised Afro-American Jug Bands, during the 1920s.

Visiting that bar, and discovering that band, was an example of the many pleasant surprises one gets when exploring Bangkok and leaves me questioning where these young kids get their ideas and inspiration.

The fashion and music explosion in Britain, during the sixties, induced a whole new world of opportunities for young people, from all kinds of social backgrounds, a revolution that was youth oriented and youth driven, and began in the streets, rather than with the old-line establishments. Suddenly, young people realised that they could excel, and become successful, and follow their dreams. Along with bands and their music, came hairdressing, photography, fashion design, modelling, pop art, and advertising, which provided opportunities to a new generation, and allowed them to express themselves with whatever strange accent they had, their family background, or what part of the country they came from. Kids from working-class families no longer felt inferior to the upper class, and the gap between them was closing.

At a time when Hollywood dominated the big screen, Sean Connery got his break as Secret British Agent James Bond 007 in 1962 and went on to play in seven James Bond films. His first job was a milkman, before joining the navy, his mother was a house cleaner, and his father worked in a factory. Michael Cain, today considered a British film icon, got his break in the sixties, and went on to make dozens of films. His father was a porter at a London fish market, and his mother a cook. Michael Caine has been personifying British cool since the swinging sixties. He has brought some of British cinema's most iconic characters to life, and introduced his very own laid-back, Cockney gangster into pop culture. He doggedly retained a regional accent, at a time when the plummy tones of Queen's English were considered obligatory. Today, his Cockney accent has become his calling card. He once said, in an interview, "*I kept my Cockney accent in order to let other working-class boys know that if I made it, they could do it too*."

Definition of a Cockney: *A native of London, especially of the working class, born in the East End, speaking a characteristic dialect of English. Traditionally defined as someone born within the sound of the bells of St Mary-le-Bow church. The current popular singer Adele is a Cockney, and proud to say, so was my mother.*

Mary Quant was a fashion designer, born in London, to Welsh parents, who were originally from mining families. After achieving a diploma in art, she went on to do an apprenticeship in fashion design, and then to open her own boutique '*bazaar*', in London's Chelsea. She had one advantage over her competitors, as she was the same age as her clients, and understood that fashion had to be affordable and assessable to a younger generation.

Wanting to provide new and interesting clothes, and not satisfied with the range of clothes available, she decided to design and stock her shop with clothes designed by herself. By 1963, she was exporting clothes to the United States, going into mass production, and the Mary Quant worldwide brand was born. During the mid-1960s, at the height of her fame, she created the micro mini skirt (that's why us men love her), although she claimed that it was the girls visiting her shops that did, as they kept wanting their skirts shorter and shorter. Later, came hot-pants, which looked ok, but guys were not so happy about them – I heard them use the words 'restricted access'! She also introduced shiny, plastic raincoats, patterned, tights and a range of cosmetics such as the 'Paint Box' makeup set. Mary's contribution to British fashion is enormous, and her influence is still felt all over the world, in clothes that young girls wear today.

It was around this time, and frequently remarked by the media, that the world's first supermodel was launched. Jean Shrimpton was widely reported to be the '*world's highest-paid model*', the '*most famous model*', *the* '*most photographed in the world*', and was described as having the '*world's most beautiful face*'. She was also dubbed '*The It Girl*', '*The Face*', '*The Face of the Moment*', and '*The Face of the '60s*'. She, and her photographer, David Bailey, transformed the fashion pages of women's magazines, as Bailey snapped Shrimpton in informal poses. Jean, herself, once remarked, years later, "If you take off the makeup, I'm ugly!" David Bailey, in the meantime, commented that he did not understand what all the fuss was about – he saw more beautiful women in the street every day.

Bailey captured and helped create the swinging London image of the 1960s' culture of fashion and celebrity chic. He has been recognised with awards from photographic societies from all over the world, and as part of the Queen's Birthday Honours, in 2001, he was awarded an OBE, the Order of the British Empire. Not bad for a kid that left school at fifteen, suffering from undiagnosed dyslexia, and a terrible school record. Despite a few dead-end jobs, he developed a love of natural history, which led him into photography. Bailey bought himself an amateur photographer's 'Box Camera', and worked as a dog's body in a studio, but went on, and continues to this day, to shoot some of the most famous celebrities in the world.

And then, there was Twiggy! Arguably, the world's first supermodel, and one that changed the face of modelling, to this day. A perfect example for any would be the scrawny, little, Asian girl model. One day, in January 1966, a skinny, little, sixteen-year-old kid, went along to Leonard's hair salon, in London's Mayfair, and over a few hours he coloured, styled, and cropped her hair. Later, they took a bus across London to meet a photographer friend of his, by the name of Barry Lategan. She had never been in front of a camera before. Lategan, spent a few hours photographing her in different poses, and rearranging her hair into different ways to show her haircut.

A few days later, Lategan made a few prints, and sent them over to Leonard, who displayed them in his Salon. A fashion journalist, from the Daily Express newspaper, saw them, and asked, "Who is this girl?" Later, she phoned to say that she wanted to meet the girl, so they both went along to her office, where she wrote an article about her, which appeared in the Daily Express, declaring Twiggy the new '*Face of '66*', and it all happened from there. By the age of seventeen, Twiggy was one of the most famous faces on the planet – her photograph was even encased in a time capsule and sent into space. Twiggy (Real name, Lesley Lawson, and nicknamed Twiggy because of her fragile stature), went on to be a successful singer, actor, writer, and a British cultural icon.

How many women can boast of marrying, not one, but two rock stars, and having songs written about them? Well, it happened to a young upcoming model, when, during 1964, she got a small part in The Beatles film, '*A Hard Day's Night*'. She only had a single line in her casting, but it resulted in her meeting, and later marrying, George Harrison. Pattie Boyd had moved to London, from the south of England, to pursue a modelling career, which later took her to Paris and New York, where she worked her way to the front of Vogue magazine. During lunch, whilst filming one day, Harrison proposed, but was turned down by Boyd, claiming she had a boyfriend at the time. When she told a friend about Harrison's approach, the response was, "*Are you completely mad? Dump your boyfriend immediately.*" So, she did, and she married Harrison in January 1966.

They spent some happy years together, until it became apparent that due to the fame, drug use, and his practice of spirituality, learning in India, George became reclusive, spending more time alone in meditation. In the meantime, George had introduced Boyd to his good friend Eric Clapton, who visited their home frequently, and so began a rock and roll triangle. Clapton grew infatuated, and she could feel it, just as she felt the lack of attention from George. One day, Clapton invited her to his apartment, saying he wanted her to listen to a song he was working on. She remarked that it was the most incredible song. It was about a man, completely obsessed by a woman, begging her to become his lover. Harrison was furious when he discovered Clapton's affection for Boyd, telling her to go off with Clapton, which she didn't until three years later, after she found out that Harrison was having an affair with Ringo Starr's wife.

Boyd married Clapton in 1979, which didn't have a happy ending either, with rumours of affairs on both sides, and Clapton's dependence on drink and drugs, and finally the arrival of a baby by another woman. They divorced in 1989. True to the sixties' rock and roll style, Clapton and Harrison remained friends up until Harrison died of cancer in 2001. Harrison once said, he would rather her marry Clapton, than some idiot! Boyd bowed out of the rock scene by marrying a property owner in 2015. Songs written about Pattie Boyd by George Harrison, and sung by The Beatles include '*Something*', and *'I Need You'*, and by Eric Clapton '*Layla*' (the one he played to her when he invited her to his apartment), and '*Wonderful Tonight*'.

In the meantime, 100 miles along the motorway, north of London, Coventry was the centre of the universe, as far as us hard-line mods were concerned.

Chapter 8
Root Values and Growing Up

If they can make penicillin out of mouldy bread, they can sure make something out of you.

Muhammad Ali.

Often, I look back, and wonder how much growing up in Coventry during the sixties has affected the rest of my life and shaped my future. Why do I do things this or that way? Why do I get annoyed or frustrated at this or that? Why am I so different to others over certain issues? Our characters obviously derive from our childhood and teenage years. As we grow older, we accept the changes to our day to day lives, without really noticing, but it is interesting and, sometimes amusing to stop and reminisce, and one can be surprised at how much life has changed (not always for the better), in ways our children will never understand.

Not many families had a TV set in their home during the early 1950s. But I remember my dad acquired a Bush TV22 set, not sure exactly when that was. It was black and white (coloured TV had not arrived at that time), nine-inch screen (my son recently ordered a 65-inch screen), set in a brown Bakelite box, made by a radio factory in London's Shepherds Bush. They cost around forty pounds sterling at the time. When turned on, it would take at least five minutes to warm up, and the picture would frequently disappear, but a firm smack on the side or the top would bring it back to life.

There were no kindergartens as such, and children's programmes were far from being educational, as they are today. I remember my younger sister and I, spending many happy afternoons, sitting on the floor, watching children's programmes, that today would probably be described as 'bizarre'. One particular programme that we enjoyed immensely (and one that I would still enjoy today because it was brilliantly crazy), was '*Bill and Ben, the Flower Pot Men*', not particularly educational, but we did learn a new language even at that age. The Flower Pot Men only spoke an inflected version of English, known as '*Oddle Poddle*'. The story revolved around two identical puppets, who lived in flowerpots at the bottom of an English garden, and a third character (a talking weed that lived between the flowerpots), named 'Little Weed'. Bill and Ben were made out of flowerpots, had large gardening gloves and hobnailed boots. They lived in terror of the gardener, and only came out when he went for lunch. They communicated in 'Oddle Poddle', and used words like '*Flobbalob*' or '*Flobbadod*', that seemed to have various meanings. 'Flopperpop', of course, meant flowerpot, and 'Loplob' meant lovely. The pair would get up to mischief, until Little Weed would warn them that the gardener was returning from lunch by a tremulous cadence of 'Weeeeeeeeed', weeeeeeeeeed which would cause them to get back in their pots, but not without saying, 'Baba pickle Weed'. You got it, 'Goodbye Little Weed'. Sometimes, for some strange reason, a tortoise would appear, and crawl silently across the screen. There were complaints at the time that kids would grow up not being able to speak correctly. Someone once described it as, "An acid trip for six-year olds." My dad would come home from work, and ask how we were doing, and get a response like, 'dobling bel Dlod' or 'gobblegog'. He would give us a strange look and say to my mum, "It's time these kids started school."

Sometimes, I wonder what the Thai people think of us *farangs*. Thais are very softly spoken, generally reserved and polite. Whereas, some of us visitors are not. So, when a loud-mouthed or drunken Brit, German or Russian goes into a bar or 7-Eleven, and asks for a big bottle of beer or something like that, and the attendant doesn't quite understand, there is a tendency to repeat the order, each time louder and louder. "Give me a big bottle of beer," assuming the louder they speak, the more the person should understand. "Noo, I said a big bottle." For the poor attendant, who doesn't have a good grasp of the English language, it must sound to them like 'Oddle Poddle'.

Without being disrespectful, I do enjoy the way some Thais pronounce English, in fact I am learning some Thai English myself, e.g. 'Fiss and Tips' is Fish and Chips, 'no spik enlik' is I don't speak English, and the letter 's' pronounced as 'sa' such as 'sa-mile', 'sa-mall' and so on. One thing I enjoy during my walks around Bangkok, is stopping in a café for a refreshing glass of 'Iced Tea'. Now, very often, the Thai waiters do not understand the order until you repeat it a few times, as the Thai's tend to pronounce Iced Tea as '*IT.*' (IT pronounced with rapid succession), and Hot Tea is pronounced as '*Hottie*'. Recently, I dropped into a street side café, and was attended by a young, enthusiastic waiter, and I confidently ordered IT., and the conversation went like this…

He thought about my order for a second, and responded, "I lemon T?"

I looked at him, and said, "No, just IT."

He quickly responded, "Okay, I apple T?"

"No," I said. "I just want IT., no lemon and no apple."

Silence for a minute, expressionless, then a slight smile, "Strawberry?"

I picked up a menu from another table, opened the drinks page, and found the iced tea list.

I showed him the list with iced lemon tea, and put my finger over the word lemon, and said, "Look, no lemon, only IT."

He nodded seriously, thought about it for a few seconds, and said, "I go get manager."

I watched the waiter go over to a smart young man, whom I assumed was the manager. They were obviously discussing the situation, as they both kept glancing in my direction. This grumpy farang had obviously disrupted their otherwise uneventful morning.

I could have happily accepted any of the iced tea flavours, but as battle had begun, I was determined to stand firm on my request.

After a few minutes, the manager strolled over to my table, and greeted me with a *sawadee kap*, how are you today, and how can I help you.

I explained that I had been trying to explain to the boy that I wanted plain IT. with no fruit flavours. At the word 'fruit flavours', the manager opened the menu, and pointed to the page, saying, "We have many flavours."

"No," I said. "No fruit flavours."

"Oh, okay, so you want hottie?"

"No, not hottie, just IT."

"Oh, I lemon T?"

Tempted to grab the manager by the throat, I calmly said, "I just want T, chai, tea with I, ice, *namkaeng*."

The manager nodded. With an expression that he finally understood, he said, "Okay IT. I will tell kitchen," and off he went.

Some minutes later, my iced tea arrived, nicely presented in a tall glass, with a sprig of mint, and a slice of lemon lodged over the top of the glass. I received it triumphantly from the waiter with a, see, I got what I wanted, look on my face, and sat back to enjoy.

Actually, it wasn't exactly what I ordered, although iced kiwi fruit tea is not that bad at all.

There was a series of other bizarre children's programmes at that time, with names such as *The Wooden Tops*, *Muffin the Mule, Rag Tag and Bobtail*, and a programme I could not get my head around, even as a young kid, called *Andy Pandy*. Andy Pandy was a puppet that lived in a picnic basket, with a teddy bear and a rag doll called Looby Loo. Somewhere in the back of my little mind, even as a five-year-old, I knew that if Andy Pandy ever grew up, he would be different to other boys. Let's just say girly.

I have fond memories of my school days at Barkers Butts Secondary Modern School. Some good things I remember, are the school dinners and the free milk in small bottles, handed out every morning. I enjoyed the bus and the walk to and from school with my friends. That's when I learned one morning, the facts of life from a boy whose parents had told him the night before. The boy appeared to still be in a state of shock, like he didn't sleep all night. I don't think I was surprised; in fact, I was happy to learn that the rumours I had heard were true. We often found discarded magazines, and the odd photo of nude women, while we were out rummaging around the countryside and back-allies, near where we lived. They were often torn into pieces, and we would spend ages joining the pieces together, and were amazed and excited with the results (and wonder why we got erections). Sometimes, someone would discover a '*johnny*' (condom) and hold it up between their fingers as a trophy. One of the older kids would shout, "Put it down, you can catch VD from those things." Us younger ones would agree, even though we had no idea what a condom or VD (venereal disease) was.

On the way home from school, there was often a fight in a back alley, between a couple of kids that had fallen out during the day and scheduled to meet after class, which put some excitement into an otherwise uneventful day.

I don't have good memories of the old-fashioned classroom clock on the wall, at the front of the class that moved so slowly, as if time was standing still, especially during the math's lesson. Calculators were not out at the time, and ballpoint pens were not allowed in schools until the late sixties, which makes me think of blotting paper! Teaching was old fashioned, where the teacher would stand at the front of the class and waffle away, whilst chalking things on the black board. The chalk was also used for throwing fiercely at any child's head if they were not paying attention. How many times was I in another world, thinking about meeting Cilla from the girl's school next door and taking her out on a date, or going to the Orchid Ballroom on the Saturday afternoon, where they had young teenage bands or played the latest music, only to wake up by being hit on the head by a flying piece of chalk? At least, when I was re-focused, the clock had moved forward by a few minutes.

In those days, it was common for teachers to hand out the cane if we misbehaved. The teachers were typical of that era (the sixties) and enforcing discipline on young lads seemed to be the top of their list of priorities, which provided them some personal satisfaction. Did caning work as a disciplinary measure? I don't think so. Did teachers gain more respect from using the cane? No way, we thought they were overpowering pathetic prats. Did caning leave any mental or physical scars? Not at all. In truth, a caning was a silent encounter between the teacher and the pupil, it was important in front of your classmates not to show any fear or emotions. After being caned, the pupil would look the teacher in the eye, and walk back to his seat, trying to show no sign of pain. He was the hero of the day, especially at break time, when the rest of the school got to know about it. After receiving the cane from the English teacher, he would always wait for me to misbehave a second time, after which, with deep satisfaction, he would shout out to the class "Oliver asking for more." *Obviously a reference to the Oliver Twist story.*

We were always told by our elders, if you want something you have to work for it. Doing a paper round, getting up in the morning at six o'clock to deliver newspapers in all weathers; wind, rain, and snow, before going to school, and again the evening papers after school was not an easy task. But I suppose that receiving a few shillings at the end of the week must have made it worthwhile. I was thirteen years of age and remember there was a lot of talk about communism around that time. I had never seen a communist, but knew there were a few around, and they were evil people, and many were Russian spies, waiting to bring our country to its knees. I would deliver a newspaper called '*The Daily Worker*' to one house, which I was told was a communist paper. I tried so hard to see the person I was delivering to, as I wanted to see what a communist really looked like, but he would never appear at the door or in the garden. I would glance in the window or look through the letterbox, but I never saw anybody from that house, which made me believe all the more that he could be a spy, up to no good, and was purposely trying to stay anonymous.

Of course, we did not have gadgets or video games, computers, internet and chat rooms, but we had a lot of friends. Today, photographs and videos can be taken with a mobile phone or digital camera, and the results examined instantly. Here is what we had to do in the sixties if we were lucky enough to own a camera.

First step was to purchase the correct type of film and install it into the camera as follows.

1. Open the back, by pulling the tag on the rewind knob.
2. Insert the film cartridge in the large open side, so that the film is coming 'over the top', as it comes out.
3. Pull the film across the camera to the other side. Depending on type of camera, either insert one end of the film into slots on the right-hand side or lay the film flat across the receiving roller that's rubber covered.
4. Make sure the film is laying across the rectangular opening in the back.
5. Close the camera until it clicks shut.
6. Wind the film until you see the rewind knob rotate. This indicates that the film is being pulled out from the cartridge and across the film window.
7. Advance the film until the counter goes to '1', and you're ready to shoot. The roll would usually stay in the camera, until the whole roll of film had been used, normally around 12 to 24 pictures, and then removed by following steps 8 to 12. The film would then be taken to the shop to be developed at more cost, and a day or two's wait in patient anticipation for the results.

Sadly, it was not uncommon when excitedly going to collect the results, to find family holiday or birthday snaps could not be developed because light had found its way into the camera, when installing or uninstalling, or the film had been slipping, and not winding over to the next frame. How disappointing was that?

Unlike today, there were very few options during the early to mid-sixties to listen to our type of music being played or watch our favourite bands, but I believe we appreciated music so much more then, than teenagers do today. Ask anyone if they remember their first vinyl album they purchased, and they will tell you the name, and probably that they saved up for three or four weeks to buy it. There was the process of flipping through record albums at the music store, studying the cover art, pulling the record out of its sleeve, flipping the record over and the big decision of which one to buy, The Small Faces or The Who, The Hollies, or Georgie Fame and the Blue Flames? Cassettes and CD's never had the same feel or value. Music today is like fast food, and so much taken for granted.

Later generations will never know the pleasures we had, of owning a vinyl LP (Long Play album). They were treasures which we could ill afford. The bands, and type of music in our collection, were a reflection of ourselves, and the designs of the album covers spoke volumes to the mind-set of each particular band, and the social commentary in their music.

Many of these album covers today are collector's items. The truly iconic album covers don't just define the album, they define an era, a generation, and expressions of a musical genre. Great album covers burn into your imagination and prepare you for the music they contain.

There are many debates and lists of what are considered to be the top all time music album covers, but the best known album cover of all time is said to be The Beatles' influential 1967 album, '*Sgt Pepper's Lonely Hearts Club Band*'. I am not sure where one would start to describe it.

The group are standing in the front of a floral garden, dressed in brightly coloured military uniforms, with mop haircuts and each sporting a moustache. Surrounding them, are cardboard cut-outs of more than seventy celebrities, with what looks like a doll of Shirley Temple on one side, wearing a Rolling Stones sweater! It's weird, and not amongst my favourites.

Also, up there with the best, and in complete contrast to their previous album covers, is The Beatles 1969 album, '*Abbey Road*', which shows the band marching in unison, across a pedestrian crossing, just outside of the EMI Studios on Abbey Road, London. The scene is very British (except for a Volkswagen car parked in the background), with John Lennon wearing a white suit, Paul McCartney, no shoes, and George Harrison bell-bottom jeans and a denim shirt. Today, four decades later, fans from all over the world visit the same spot to recreate the picture, featuring themselves. But, of course, they don't have the traffic police, out of site of the camera, holding up the traffic to assist the photographer!

Cover album art, at times, became very controversial, such as Van Halen's 1984, '*Jump*' album, which featured a very sweet baby angel sitting innocently, with a lit cigarette in its hand and two packs of cigarettes. on the table in front of him. The cover was censored in the UK at the time of the album's release, with a sticker that obscured the cigarette in the child's hand and the packs of cigarettes.

One of the most recognisable album covers of all time is Nirvana's 1991 album, '*Nevermind*'. Not only was the music original, so was the cover art. The cover featured a naked four-month-old baby, submerged in deep, blue water, his baby penis sticking out from under his little belly, and arms reaching out to grab a dollar bill attached to a fishing line and fishhook. The parents of the boy, 'Spencer Eldon', were paid the equivalent to £154.00 for one of the most well-known album covers in history, and an album that went on to sell over 30 million copies worldwide.

There is the nostalgia, as well as the ritual. We would visit friends' houses and play each other's music, listening carefully to the words, often re-playing over and over again, arguing over the lyrics and meaning of the songs. We would proudly carry our albums under our arms, hoping others would see what we owned, and what music or bands we were into. My friend, Johnny Gibbins, would arrive at my house with a Spencer Davies Group album or The Yardbirds, and we would play them in the back room for hours. I would visit him with my The Rolling Stones or Georgie Fame and the Blue Flames.

One of the most creative long-lasting partnerships in modern music started like that, in 1960, when two old schoolmates bumped into each other on the platform of Dartford railway station. One of them was carrying some R&B records, amongst them Chuck Berry and Muddy Waters vinyl long players. The music that Mick Jagger was carrying, revealed a common interest as Keith Richards grandfather played with a jazz band. They would frequently meet at Jagger's house, and so began a musical partnership, before forming a quintet, calling themselves the Blues Boys. Later, with the Rolling Stones, they started to write their own songs, going on to sell millions worldwide.

One of my greatest regrets is that I never learned to play an instrument or was able to sing when I was growing up. But music over the years has followed me everywhere and is very important to me today. Sadly, popular music has become such a lucrative industry, and corporations invest so much in it that songs are peddled on radio stations, and by way of videos knowing the more it's repeated, the more it repeats in our heads. Music today is a multi-billion-dollar industry, and we are being held captive and force-fed music sung by superficial propped-up performers. There is very little individuality. I have no particular favourite types of music, in fact, I enjoy most types. Music is our own experiences and thoughts and can depend on one's mood and reminds us of people and places of times past. Music develops photographs of days gone by in the mind.

I remember summer holidays with my mates, during the sixties hanging out, chasing girls and exploring the pubs in coastal towns, such as Newquay and Torquay, whenever I hear The Beatles', '*Hey Jude*' and '*All You Need is Love*'.

We would bum a lift with other guys we knew, that were going down that way, that were happy for us to contribute to the cost of the petrol. It was amazing how many of us could fit inside a small Mini Minor or a Hillman Imp car.

During the seventies, working aboard Banana Boats, visiting small towns, surrounded by jungle in and around central and South American countries, we would drink in small seaman-type girly bars, and for some reason the juke boxes always played Barry White's '*Can't Get Enough of Your Love, Babe*' and '*Mississippi*', by the band Pussycat. I can still see and smell those wonderful sleazy little bars, when I hear those songs now, and remember the laughs we had, trying to converse with those crazy bar girls. It was in one of those bars, that I learned the art of making friends, when an American seaman walked over to our table, with a beer in his hand, sat down, and said, "Hi, do you mind if I join you guys, and shoot the shit for an hour or two?"

Around that time, back in the UK, every parent and schoolteacher's nightmare 'The Sex Pistols', featuring Johnny Rotten and Sid Vicious, were giving us hell with their Punk Rock. I loved it, even though some of my shipmates thought I was becoming a bit old for the Punk Scene.

The eighties, falling in love with, and spending our hard earnings on Brazilian girls in the Discos, around Rio de Janeiro to Michael Jackson '*Billy Jean*', or Donna Summer's '*Hot Stuff*', and then there were the nineties, watching the live bands around Dubai, attempting to play Oasis' '*Wonderwall*', or Guns and Roses' '*November Rain*'.

Music is also medicine, once described as 'what feelings sound like', so why waste money on psychotherapy when music is medicine of the mind. Even dairy cows enjoy music, apparently it was discovered that when their favourite song, '*Everybody Hurts*' by R.E.M., appears they produce more milk.

And what about good old-fashioned country music, played on a few cords, and saying it exactly how it is. Your woman has left you for another man, you got fired from your job and you are down on your luck. Nothing better than sitting at the bar on your own, staring at the bottom of your beer glass, and listening to Hank Williams Snr singing, '*Your*

Cheating Heart', or '*I'm So Lonesome I Could Cry*', and letting your emotions flow, or just take the opera singer as an example, he gets stabbed in the back, and instead of dying, he breaks into song.

Chapter 9
Coventry Days

For those who are lost, there will always be cities that feel like home.

Simon Van Booy.

I was sitting at the bar the recently, browsing on my phone, as we tend to do these days, and came across the following review on Trip Advisor, which had the heading '*Coventry should not be on any Tourist Map*'. The review was submitted by someone under the name of '*bobswinarski*'. This is what he wrote, quote:

"*I'll say it again. Coventry is an ugly dirty, beat-up broken-down violent shit hole that is definitely far off any tourist map. I can see no other reason to go there other than to gaze at the mire of its post-industrial landscape of bordered up factories and weed-strewn car parks, it's a wretchedly horrible place with some of the ugliest samples of the human species on record.*

It's ugly

It's littered strewn and dirty.

It smells like ass

It's bleak

It's depressing

It's dire.

The inhabitants are largely dirty, nose picking uneducated, ignorant, loud-mouthed drunken rabble. Watch them they bite! Worst of all they are extremely unfriendly and wary of anybody not from 'Cov'. Public drunkenness and prostitution seem to be the major pastimes of the female population. 'So there, send that to Fodor!'" Unquote.

Not all our friend said is true, Coventrians do not bite visitors, at least I don't think they do. They do, however, support freedom of expression and speech, so all we can say is, "Fuck you, you foreign git." Today, Coventry is the fastest-growing city in Britain, north of London, mainly due to international migration and acceptance of refugees, who seem quite happy to take advantage of everything this beat-up, broken-down, violent, shithole has to offer. We should not forget, Coventry was devastated during World War Two, and had to start again, and its people rebuilt their lives, just like the refugees today!

One morning some time ago, I was walking close to my accommodation in Bangkok, when a friendly, local Thai gentleman wished me good morning, stopped, and asked me where I came from. I explained that I came from a city in England called Coventry and asked him if he knew it. He replied, laughing, that he didn't know it, but had been sent to Coventry many times. I was surprised that he knew the phrase, '*Sent to Coventry*'. He knew what it meant but had no idea where it originated. To send someone to Coventry is an English idiom, meaning to deliberately ostracise someone. Typically, this is done by not talking to them, avoiding someone's company, and generally pretending that they no longer exist. Victims are treated as though they are completely invisible and inaudible.

I explained to my new friend that it is believed that the origin dates back to the English Civil War (1642-49), Coventry was a strong Parliamentarian town. Due to this, Royalist soldiers, stationed in or near Coventry, would be totally ignored by the locals. Excluded from taverns and all merrymaking in general, royalists would be forced to endure a very miserable existence. As a result, the term, to be sent to Coventry, came to mean to be excluded from events or to be a social outcast. My Thai friend went on his way quite happily.

At least we were not sent to Coventry, my parents moved there from a neighbouring village when we kids were still young, and how lucky we were.

On December 7th, 2017, Coventry was named as the UK's City of Culture 2021, which is a great achievement, following the years of suffering, since the decline of the car industry.

Recently, after forty years of living abroad, I spent some time in Coventry. How much I enjoyed wandering around the older parts of the city, amongst the 14th century buildings that survived Hitler's bombs. I visited old pubs, historical buildings with small rooms and log fires, selling all types of real ales, all of which I just took for granted when I was a young man growing up there. I discovered that the factory I worked at all those years ago has been replaced by a Hypermarket and McDonalds. Jaguar cars are now owned by Tata of India, and Carbodies, (London Taxis) that went into decline, were bailed out by the Chinese. On visiting the old Central Post Office, I found it now to be called '*Wah Yan Hong Oriental Food Specialists*', and later found the Post Office situated inside '*Smith's Book Shop*'. The Locarno Ballroom, where me and my mates spent so many nights posing at the bar, trying to impress girls with our mod culture, and where we saw many great rock bands, is now the City Central Library, the City Arms Pub next door, where we sat drinking one night with '*The Singing Postman*' is a charity shop. The once-famous Hotel Leofric, where many famous people stayed over the years, is now accommodation for foreign students. The city has become a university city. The streets were awash with Asian students.

I wonder how many people remember the Saturday '*Tanner Rush*; in the 60s. In those days, a sixpenny piece was called a tanner, and every Saturday morning hordes of snotty-nose, scruffy, little kids, with their younger brothers, sisters, mini gangs and hooligans from all parts of the city, would flock to the local cinema which cost a '*tanner*' to enter. It was not just the films that we enjoyed, it was complete bedlam from going down to the city on the old corporation bus with a crowd of our friends, to being let loose from parents, teachers, and adults in general. If I remember, it was called the *ABC Minors Club* (I believe it was in cinemas every Saturday morning, countrywide). Hundreds of kids would cause havoc in the foyer of the cinema, trying to sneak their younger brothers or sisters in for free under the turnstile, or through the curtains at the entrance to the theatre, which would leave them extra money to buy ice cream at the interval. Others would pay to go in, then open the fire door or exit doors, with their friends waiting to come in from the outside. There was a manager called 'uncle', someone or other, whose job it was to manage the show, and his lady assistants, who were, I suppose, 'usherettes', that went through hell, trying to control hundreds of little brats every week. Before the films started, uncle would stand on the stage, in front of the screen, in a black dinner suit with his black Bryl-creamed hair and moustache, winding the kids up and get them to sing the ABC Minors song. Those who were members of the ABC Minors Club had badges, and on their birthday, would have their names read out, and go on the stage to receive a small gift, to the boos of scores of kids. When joining the club, kids would lie about their birthday, so they didn't have to wait too long for a free gift. There would be an interval when the usherettes would stand at the front, with trays selling ice cream and orange juice. Sometimes, the film projector would stutter and stop, throwing the theatre into darkness, resulting with the booing and stamping of feet, and empty ice cream, orange juice cups and chewing gum flying all over the place, which would stop immediately the film recommenced. The show normally started with cartoons, followed by the main film which would be American, such as *Flash Gordon*, *Zorro*, *The Lone Ranger* or *Hopalong Cassidy*, and would run for a number of weeks. At the end of each instalment, the hero would find himself in an impossible situation, like falling off the edge of a cliff, being run over by a train, or crushed by an enormous rock rolling towards him. Just as he was about to breath his last breath, an announcement would appear on the screen such as *'Can the Lone Ranger escape? What can he do? Come back next week to find out what happens'.* After waiting all week, you would return, and find that the train was not travelling as fast or the rock was not quite so close to your hero as it appeared before, and he would simply roll out of the way, and the story would continue. There would be a mad rush for the exits the second the film ended, only to find that they were blocked by uncle and the usherettes, forcing the kids to stand and wait for the national anthem to finish.

Chapter 10
The Factory Worker

If England became a world power, it was because of the industrial revolution.

N R Narayana Murthy.

The first British car was built in Coventry by Daimler in 1879. Coventry's manufacturing industry grew until it reached a peak in the 1960s. At that time, the UK was the second-biggest car maker in the world, and a host of the major companies were based in and around Coventry, including the British Motor Corporation (maker of the mini, Morris Minor), Jaguar, Standard-Triumph, Carbodies (assembled the London Taxis), Triumph Motor Cycles, Massey Ferguson Tractors, to name a few. During that time, the average wage in Coventry was 25% higher than the rest of the country.

I joined the Alvis car factory as an apprentice toolmaker. The Alvis was a company that assembled five cars a week in 1965, together with building a number of types of armoured military vehicles and aero engines. "Get a trade behind you lad, you can't go wrong," they said. "Then, when you finish your apprenticeship, you can get a mortgage, buy a house and get married."

"Get what?" I said.

So, while I was an apprentice, earning £7 to £10 a week, the un-skilled guys, on the assembly lines or in the machine shops, were earning up to £40 a week, buying cars and houses, and putting money in the bank. Five years later, when I finished my time, and received my indentures for completing my apprenticeship, it was obvious that those industrial trades such as toolmaker, pattern maker, copper smith etc., were becoming obsolete. And so, I left the factory, and went to sea, working on merchant ships as an engineer.

They were happy times. I made new friends, both from the factory, and at the technical college, which we attended one day and one evening each week. Attached to the factory, was a sports ground and a working men's club, that belonged to the Alvis. As apprentices, we would work to gain experience in the different sections of the factory, such as the machine shop, assembly line, quality control, inspection of parts etc., and finally for me, the tool room. The one thing that surprised me on starting work, was how immature, vulgar, and sometimes stupid, adults could be, which somewhat changed my opinion of them. I would look at my Uncle Gilbert, who worked for Coventry Transport and visited us on a Sunday, and wonder if he ever grabbed young apprentices by the balls for a joke. Our next-door neighbour Mr Hazell, who worked at the Standard Car Factory; did he sneak off to the toilets with pornographic magazines, stuffed down his shirt? And what about my father who worked at Jaguar? What if he insisted on telling everyone in hearing distance, how much he would like to screw big fat Molly, who worked in the pay office. Having said that, most of my superiors, during my apprenticeship, were very patient, unselfish and generous when it came to teaching, and passing on their knowledge to a young man, like myself.

Spending some apprenticeship time in a factory meant access to stories of, and working together with a number of strange characters, which was an education in itself. As I moved around the various departments, the more intrigued I became. There was an elderly gentleman in the tool room, who would march into the workshop, stand to attention and salute his machine, before starting work every morning. Another saggy, sad-faced gentleman would approach me, and secretly hand me a pornographic magazine to read when I visited the washroom. Later, he would come over and ask my opinion of the contents. He would make comments like, "Good photography, wasn't it?", "The photographer got the angles and lighting right, didn't he?", "Good quality paper," etc. I, of course, did not notice any of that. It just got me praying for the weekend to come, and that I might find a piece of skirt who needed some adult entertainment with a smart young guy like me, who knew everything about sex. This same gentleman drove a Volkswagen Beetle, which I thought was quite provocative, given that we were working in the car industry in Coventry, and it was Adolf Hitler (who destroyed our city) that promoted the Beetle in Germany as 'the People's Car', during the mid-thirties.

I observed that when the workers were not reading porn magazines or talking about sex, sport or politics, some would read children's comic magazines at lunch and break times. The 1960s was possibly the golden age of children's comics. Children (and some adults) would look forward to Thursdays and Fridays, when the new editions came out. There were dozens to choose from for all ages, for both boys and girls. A comic is described as a publication that consists of comic art, in the form of coloured sequential juxtaposed panels that represent individual scenes, often accompanied by a brief descriptive of the topic or speech balloons. A number of magazines, that I recall, which were very popular then, are '*Beano*', and '*The Dandy*', and for older kids, '*Eagle*', and '*Valiant*', all of which bring back vivid memories, which are hard to describe. The characters were fascinating, and the stories stretched the imagination. For easy reading I enjoyed more, the simple characters, *Eagle* and *Valiant* were a little more serious.

When comics were invented sometime before the nineteen forties, they were one of the few things to entertain many children, up until the sixties. Each comic book had any number of stories, around different characters, and each had their particular hero. The Dandy, if I remember, had 'Desperate Dan', hailed as the world's strongest and toughest man. He can lift a horse with one arm, he shaves with a blow torch, and likes nothing better than to tuck into an enormous cow pie (with the horns sticking out of the pastry), made for him by his Aunt Aggie. Dan hails from the Wild West town of '*Cactusville*'. Dan was originally a rogue, that later became friendly by helping the town folk of 'Cactusville'. There is a life size statue of Dan and his dog name 'Dawg' (the hardest hound around), in the centre of the city of Dundee, Scotland, that attracts lots of visiting children, and a few adults too (that most likely grew up in the sixties).

The star of Beano was 'Dennis the Menace', known for his distinctive red and black jumper, outsized shoes and devilish grin. This spiky-haired kid and his partner in crime, 'Gnasher' the dog, are as ante as can be. Denis is a loner, and is often armed with a catapult, peashooter or water pistol, to terrorise other boys his age or ambush the postman. He enjoys scaring girls, by taking a frog or slug from his pocket, and making them scream. While most of his mischief is for fun, sometimes it can cause serious problems, and his antics have caused him to gain multiple enemies including his neighbours, the 'Colonel', who lives across the road, and 'Sergeant Slipper', the policeman.

Sadly, over the decades, the antics that children are allowed to do has changed considerably, as have punishments. The beatings, or slipperings, that Denis received from his dad, and his wild antics, I imagine that, if in fact Dennis is still around today, are not portrayed as so evil, and the stories have a less anti-establishment tone. Poor kids today don't know what they are missing! The Eagle and the Valiant characters were more mature, educational and futuristic, and featured characters such as 'Dan Dare, Pilot of the Future, and 'Captain Hurricane'.

As apprentices, we were allowed to use the sports ground facilities for a couple of hours, two mornings a week, where we normally played football. Annually, the factory arranged inter-departmental competitions, games of football or cricket between teams, put together by the different departments that were held in the evenings after work. It was hilarious, watching some of the football games such as the squeaky-clean 'Ho Ho Harry' office workers, against the 'rough-ass maintenance department', who in spite of their ages, and lack of physical fitness were determined to do what it took to win the competition. Cramps, foot and leg injuries were common together, with the odd exchange of punches and head butts, assisted with some un-repeatable language. The reserves on the bench didn't have to wait long to get their chance to play, and teams rarely finished with eleven players, after a few red cards had been handed out. But all was forgotten a couple of hours later, when the teams and their supporters got together for a few pints of beer in the factory's working-man's club. I turned out one time for the apprentice cricket team and can proudly boast a score of not out for one run.

Apprentice educational day trips were sometimes arranged, to tour other factories or visit exhibitions that were of interest. I remember a trip to visit the first Concord, Supersonic Passenger Aircraft that was being built by the British Aircraft Corporation in Bristol England, whilst at the same time, one was being constructed by SUD Aviation in Toulouse France. We also had a few trips to London, such as a tour of the Ford car assembly plant at Dagenham, and the annual Motor Show. The trips to London we enjoyed the most, as when the visit was over, we had free time to ourselves to explore the city, before re-joining the rest of the guys to catch the coach back to Coventry around midnight. For that reason, a few of us would try and make the visits to the establishments as short as possible, or if it was an exhibition just disappear. There are, of course, many things to see and do in London, such as Buckingham Palace, The Houses of Parliament, art galleries, museums, and so on. But those places are for tourists. For a group of seventeen to twenty-year-old factory workers visiting London, there were better places to visit, such as first on the list, 'pubs'.

The Blind Beggar Pub on Whitechapel Road was on the top of our list. It was outside this pub, that sometime during 1865, William Booth preached a sermon, which created The Salvation Army, a Protestant Christian Church and international charitable organisation, which was structured in military fashion to bring salvation to poor, destitute and hungry people. But we visited for another reason. We had all read and heard stories about the notorious Kray Twins, and it was here in the saloon bar, that on 9th March 1966, Ronnie

Kray, in front of witnesses in the bar (who at the identification parade, said they didn't recognise him), shot and murdered George Cornell, an associate of a rival gang, who was sitting at the bar. Cornell had apparently called Kray, who was a known bisexual, 'a fat poof', some days earlier. (Ronnie had been exposed by a tabloid newspaper, insinuating that he had a sexual relationship with Robert, Lord Boothby, a Conservative politician, at a time when being gay was still a criminal offence). Upon hearing of his location, Ronnie drove over from a nearby pub, and they say that Cornell's last words, as Kray approached him were, "Well, look who's here." The jukebox, which also took a bullet at the time, was playing '*The Sun Ain't Going to Shine Anymore*', by the Walker Brothers. The Kray twins, and their gang, known as '*The Firm*', were involved in organised crime, in and around the East End of London, during the 1960s. The gang were notorious for their part in murder, armed robbery, and protection rackets. The Krays owned a West End nightclub, where they entertained prominent politicians and celebrities, such as Frank Sinatra and Judy Garland. For a time, they were seen by the establishment as prosperous and charming, and part of the swinging London scene.

Also, on our list was the 'Prospect of Whitby', reputed to be the oldest pub on the Thames riverside, dating back to 1520. In former times, it was a meeting place for sailors, smugglers and cut-throats. Over the years, it has been visited by royalty, and many famous stars and celebrities. The writers Charles Dickens and Samuel Pepys are known to have been regulars there. It seems that Charles Dickens used to visit most of the old London pubs in his time. I remember we would take the London Tube to the Wapping Station and walk to it along some narrow-cobbled streets, between old unlit warehouses but I don't remember much about the return journey. In the evenings, it was very crowded, the beer flowed, and the crowds sang along to those old-fashioned pub '*singsong*' songs, to a band playing Hawaiian guitars. On our visits to London, we spent many happy evenings there.

Some years later, whilst visiting my daughter, who was at university in London, at the time, I took her to the Prospect of Whitby for (I think, a Sunday) lunch and thought I would impress her with my knowledge of places to visit in London. Places are never quite the same as you remember them, and Britain is certainly not known for its catering etiquette. It was strange (after living so many years abroad), not to be waited on in a restaurant or bar. Instead, the dishes would be placed on the bar, and you would collect your order yourself. An unshaved, Aussie bartender would let customers know when the food was ready, by shouting out at the top of his voice, "Who ordered the T-bone steak, well done, with wedges, and a double portion of onions?", and a few minutes later, "Who ordered a king-size burger, with fries and tomato relish?" then, "Who ordered the spaghetti…?" On it went, all through the lunchtime period.

We would take a walk along Carnaby Street, in the West End of London, which became a household name all around the world, because of its influences on London's fashion during the sixties. Many of the mod-style clothes, worn by members of the top groups, such as the Kinks, The Who and the Rolling Stones, were designed in Carnaby Street, and so it became intertwined with Britain's music culture. But, our main purpose to be in that area was to explore Soho, the home, during that time, of recording studios, nightclubs, seedy strip clubs and sex shops. We would wander through the cul-de-sacs and back alleys and be aroused to see the prostitutes, standing in doorways, beckoning passers-by for business. Others would pin ambiguous messages at the entrance, to where they served their clients, advertising their services, such as, 'come in and visit Gloria for French lessons'. One time, curiosity got the better of us, and with my friend, we crept down some creaking winding wooden stairs, and knocked on the door of one of these secretive discreet establishments. The door opened slightly, and a scantily dressed lady looked through the door, and said, in a not so friendly voice, "Yes, what do you want?" My friend answered, "We have come for French lessons." With a horrible glare, she looked us up and down, and replied, loudly, "Then fuck off, and find them somewhere else." And, we scarpered back up the stairs. I think it was the first time I heard a woman swear like that.

We would have a beer in the notorious Dog and Duck pub and pool our money to see if we had enough to visit a strip club. The sleazy strip clubs that we could afford were below street level, down a winding staircase in a small, darkened room, but frequented by elderly city gentlemen in pin-striped suits and bowler hats. The strippers would appear from behind a curtain and perform on a small stage, with a crackling sound system for the background music, that left a lot to be desired. The strippers were not particularly exciting and very serious, some danced naked, but with enormous bouquets of peacock feathers in their hands, which they manoeuvred to cover their private parts with every twist and turn of the dance, which finally ended with them putting their arms in the air to show a full frontal for about three seconds, before the lights being dimmed, and the girl disappearing behind the curtain.

The sex shops were interesting, but the books were sealed in cellophane, the blow-up dolls were amusing, and the sex toys confusing. It was obvious to the sales staff we were not serious customers, so it was not long before we were asked to leave.

And so, our intended educational day trips to London ended on the coach back to Coventry. If we did not learn very much professionally, we certainly made up for it socially.

One of our educational trips was a tour of the Mitchel & Butlers Brewery in Birmingham, which was probably not a good idea. It was boring, and we ended up sampling more beers than we should have. A snowball fight developed, throwing foam at each other, from that which accumulates around at the top of the large vats that store the beer. Our company was informed of our misbehaviour and advised that we would not be invited back for further visits.

Looking back now, it's difficult to remember how we maintained contact with friends and family, or how we made and kept appointments given that, at the time we had none of the gadgets of communication which are available today. The differences in technology, living standards and how we live have changed drastically. A lot of what we did was planned days ahead or passed on by word of mouth. If we arrived in the pub or club late, the barman would pass on messages such as Brian and Mick were in, but went to the City Arms, a couple of the other lads said they would be in the Town Wall Tavern.

During the sixties, a home telephone was still regarded as a luxury item in Britain. For many people, public telephone kiosks were their only experience of using a phone. It was sometime in 1968 that we became the proud owners of a home phone, which for some reason was placed on a stand in the hall, just in front of the front door. I don't know why, but most homes in Britain placed their phones in the hall, just inside the front door. The phone was, of course, a novelty when first installed, and each one of us would be waiting for it to ring, just for the joy of answering it. We were not encouraged to use it or spend time chatting on it, because of the call charges that were billed monthly. In the evenings, after work, we would have dinner and settle down in the back room, in front of the TV, smoke a cigarette, watch the regional news, and soap operas such as '*Cross Roads*', or '*Emmerdale Farm*', and have a nap. By sods law, just as I was dropping off, someone would say, "Is that the phone ringing?", and in unison we would say, "It's all right, I'll get it." Normally it wasn't ringing, it was wishful thinking. People, in those days, always answered the phone by giving their number first, and then their name. My mother, who had a strong Cockney accent, from one day to the next, developed a posh telephone accent that sounded more like the Queen Mother. I smile today, when I remember, "This is Coventry 79716, Vera speaking." It was fine for a while, except that we had an elderly, Aunty Phyllis who lived alone, and got into the habit of ringing in the evenings, just for someone to talk to. She would always call around the time that I was waiting for a call from one of my mates to tell me where and at what time we were meeting later. Now, Aunty Phyllis would spend a very long time on the phone, chatting about nothing at all and the family got wise to the time she would phone, so would sit tight when the phone rang. I would try and wait them out, but finally had to answer it, in case it was one of the lads trying to call me. I would listen to her for what seemed ages, and then say, "I will see if mums around," and my mum would politely tell me she wasn't, after some time I would interrupt her, and say, "I will see where dad is," only to be told by dad with a smile, sitting back in the arm chair smoking a cig, that he was busy, and so I would spend many hours listening to aunty Phyllis's visits to the doctor, her swollen ankles, that she had been to the shop and forgot to buy eggs, and she was getting a chill because of a draft coming in under the door, that she went to the post office to send a letter and forgot her purse, and so on. My father, when he thought I had suffered long enough, would finally appear in the hall with a smirk on his face, and thankfully relieve me of my plight.

The generation that grew up during the sixties had a better appreciation of, and were more careful with, money, probably because the advertising and marketing campaigns were not so prominent, and were not in our heads, telling us how we should part with it. Neither did the media control what they believed we needed, should have, and how we should look, as they do today, in just about everything money can buy. We were not as materialistic, and the different classes were respected for what they were. There was no self-pity, no hang-ups, and no inferiority complex. We were working class. There was no shame in that. It was what we were. There was a genuine sense of community, which I fear many people today have never experienced. We did not spend money on luxuries we could ill afford, such as expensive meals, exclusive nightclubs, watches, jewellery, etc., or ordering taxis to take us wherever we wanted to go. We would walk, or take the corporation bus, or both. How many times did I walk the three or four miles home in all kinds of weather after a night out? How many times did I walk a girl home to the other side of town, praying I would get something in return for my efforts, only to be rebuffed at her doorstep, and face the long walk home? Of course, the following day when the lads questioned me on how I got on the previous night, I would just wink with a shit-eating grin, and say, "I'm not telling you."

It was not uncommon for the police, who were on duty, to stop people they came across in the early hours, and ask them their name, what they had been doing, where they were going, and where they lived. I suppose today's 'political correctness' prevents them from doing this and would be interpreted as racialist or anti-something, or other. I had a friend who had been out on the town, and after a few drinks, was staggering home, when he was stopped by a police constable, who asked him his name, and where he was going. His name is made up of the two the most common English names, which is 'Tom and Smith'. The conversation went like this…

"Good morning, son, do you mind telling me where you are going at this time of the morning, and giving me your name?"

"I am going home, I live in Earlsdon, and my name is Tom Smith."

"What did you say your name is?"

"It's Tom Smith."

"Come on, Son, I think you can do better than that, what's your real name?"

"It's what I told you, Tom Smith."

"Listen son, I have been in the police force for more than twenty years, I am not stupid, and I know when someone is not telling me the truth."

"Okay, it's Elvis Presley."

"That's better, well Elvis, make your way straight home, and stay out of trouble, good night."

One of the hurdles one had to cross after a night out around the city centre, if not going on to a club or a party, was the decision on whether to take 'the last bust home'. The pubs would stop serving alcohol at 10.30 p.m. and allowed ten minutes drinking up time, before closing the doors. The last buses from the city centre would leave at 11.00 p.m. Catching the last double-decker Coventry Corporation bus home was a lottery, in that one never knew what was going to happen. It could be fun, humorous, scary, or troublesome, depending which characters or nutters were on, or got on the bus, where they had been, and how much alcohol they had consumed. Many of the regulars, that took the last bus, would have been excellent candidates for the *Jeremy Kyle Show*.

Normally, when boarding a bus, one tends to choose an empty seat, as it is not considered normal or polite to sit next to a stranger, if there are empty seats available. Just as it's not normal to start a conversation with a stranger in the toilet, when one is standing next to him at the urinal. However, on boarding the 'last bus', a decision had to be made, i.e. do I sit next to a normal, sober-looking passenger, and relax, or do I sit alone, and take a chance on who might board the bus and sit next to me, as it fills up on the route home? As it always did. Often, a couple of regular rowdy passengers, near the front, looking down out of the window from the top deck, would give a running commentary on who was standing at each bus stop, waiting to board the bus, "Yes, Taffy is getting on,"; "Oh no, it's that weird Ben Leach guy,"; "It's that big, red-haired Scotsman again, he looks drunk." One could hear them coming up the stairs, and you would pray to yourself, *please don't sit next to me*. You could sense the other passengers' relief when the nut case chose not to sit next to them. Their anxiety would turn to morbid amusement, when they sat back and watched some unlucky passenger, having an uncomfortable rapport with a nutter, which often happened to be me! How did it feel when that big Scotsman, with the Glaswegian accent, chose to sit next you and started a slurred conversation, which you didn't understand a word he said, so you just nodded each time he nudged you, and said, "Aye laddie, do ya kin?" And things like that, you would laugh when he laughed, pretending to understand his jargon, hoping not to upset him. Big, fat Taffy, when he came upstairs, would go to the front of the bus, look back, and in his beautiful Welsh accent shout, "Yaki dar boyo's, who wants a song?", to which the response from the passengers was normally

"Nooo", and he would break into Engelbert Humperdink's song, '*Please Release Me, Let Me Go*'.

The characters one had to avoid were the aggressive ones that might be looking for a fight, just to round off their night out. There was a neighbour of mine, who took pleasure in threatening guys younger than himself. You normally knew when he was getting on the bus, as you could hear him shouting things like, "Are you trying to push in boy? You'll be sorry when I've finished with you." He would get off the bus at the same bus stop as me, and usually find some reason to threaten me about something. My mother always said that he seemed quite a nice boy, until he fell off his bike and banged his head on the road when he was a kid. By the time the bus arrived at my stop, Taffy could be heard singing Humperdink's '*I Had the Last Waltz with You*'.

Engelbert Humperdink is an English traditional pop singer, real name Arnold George Dorsey, born in Leicester England, and sold more than 150 million records worldwide.

There were times when we would get a tip off that someone had 'an empty house', and was throwing a party, "But don't tell anyone I told you." Well, of course, we wouldn't tell anyone. Except a couple of mates, that were also looking for somewhere to go when the pub closed. Sometimes, parents would go away, and leave their innocent teenage son or daughter to look after the house for a few days, while they were away.

Now, nobody in their right mind would throw a party in their own home and let strangers or a crowd of yobbo's like us in, but they did, whether they liked it or not. We would gate crash the party with some smooth talk at the door, saying we were friends of the host, let's say 'Gordon', and he said we could pop around for an hour on the way home, etc. Once inside, we would mingle and chat to anyone and everyone so the guests thought we were friends of the host and the host thought we were friends of the guests, of course we were city mods dressed very smart in our suits, with collars and ties and fresh haircuts, so some of the kids were happy to hang out and chat with us. Slowly, we would make our way to the kitchen where the booze was normally stowed and take advantage of whatever was available.

Everything would be fine for a couple of hours, guys would chat up and pair off with the girls, the record player would be blasting out music, such as the Spencer Davies Group's '*Keep on Running',* The Small Faces' '*Itchycoo Park*', or the Animals' '*It's my Life*'. Slowly, the booze would start taking effect, the guests would become a little rowdy, and couples get aroused, dancing, snogging and sneaking upstairs into the bedrooms.

About this time, Gordon, who was a little worse for wear, having had a few drinks himself, was starting to get nervous. He was suggesting to the guests that it was getting late and time to leave. It did, of course, fall on deaf ears, and the typical response was,

"Gordon fuck off, the party's just starting."

Gordon could be heard banging on the bedroom doors that were locked from the inside, by couples borrowing the beds for a quick shag.

"Open the frigging doors, I said nobody was allowed upstairs, who's in my parent's room? Get out."

To a mute response from those inside.

Gordon appeared in the living room with an empty whiskey bottle in one hand and rum bottle in the other.

"Which bastards raided my dad's drinks cabinet, and drank all the booze? That's his finest Scottish Grouse Whiskey, it costs a fortune, and he's gonna fucking kill me."

Gordon could be seen on his hands and knees, with a bowl of soapy water, trying to clean red wine spilled on the sheepskin rug in front of the fire,

"Holy shit, the stain won't come out. What am I going to tell my mum? She loves this rug. Which fucking idiot did this?"

Gordon is shaking and trying to wake some guy laid out on the sofa, fast asleep, with his dirty shoes on, to no avail.

"Who is this fucking dickhead anyway, who invited him?"

Nobody had any idea who the guy is!

Suddenly, an enormous bang from the bedroom above, and Gordon rushes up the stairs. "What was that noise? What happened?"

Silence from inside.

"What the fuck was that noise? What happened? I'm going to call the police."

"Sorry Gordon, the bed collapsed, there's only four of us on it!"

Apart from a few bodies lying asleep around the house, and a couple of Gordon's friends staying behind to help him clean up, we, together with the guests, drifted away in the early hours to make our way home. A good night was had by all, except for Gordon, that is!

I can recall a party that we gate crashed one evening, after the pubs closed, when over a few drinks, I got chatting to one of the guests, a very sweet girl. It was all going well, and I was giving it my best, trying to appear smooth and intelligent. We were getting on fine, when she surprised me, and suggested that we go outside together for a while and get some fresh air. My luck was in. We stood in the garden, chatting and smooching for a while. I was becoming horny; in a way any young guy of that age will tell you. I felt she was yielding to my attempts of wooing her into some sexual activity, so suggested we go and sit in my friend's car for a while. She readily agreed, and, like an expert, I put the front seats forward (it was a small Hillman Imp) and helped her into the back seat. Everything was fine, for a while, until she started to become agitated, I asked if she was all right. She looked me in the eyes, and was trying to say something when suddenly, *her face turned ghostly, a whiter shade of pale*, before proceeding to vomit all over the back of the car! My main concern, of course, was my pigskin brogues and blue-serge trousers, but thankfully they escaped, except for a few small splashes of wine-smelling vomit. The carpets got most of it, together with some un-chewed carrots and tomato and whatever else she had taken from the buffet table.

Now, I don't remember if I left my good friend Chick (Mick), the owner of the car, to clean up the mess. But if I did, and you ever read this, Chick, I am truly sorry.

Chapter 11
The Music and Those Who Inspired Me

My music fights against the system that teaches to live and to die.

Bob Marley.

Although rock and roll became popular in the 1950s, it wasn't until the early sixties, and the sudden appearance of groups like The Beatles, the Rolling Stones and The Who, and in America, Bob Dylan, The Doors and The Beach Boys, that music began its revolutionary change. This was a turning point in music, which inspired other musicians to experiment with new individual sounds and develop innovative pieces of music. A number of singers and bands, at that time, used their music to encourage rebellion against the authorities and to encourage young people to stand up for their beliefs and individuality.

Around this period, British music was getting recognised in the USA and became known as The British Invasion. In February 1964, when The Beatles visited America for the first time and took the country by storm, the term Beatlemania was coined, and Britain began to rule the airwaves with artists such as Herman's Hermits, The Animals, The Kinks, The Who, The Yardbirds, Gerry and the Pacemakers, The Moody Blues, The Hollies, Cilla Black, Dusty Springfield, to name a few. When The Beatles visited the USA, Life Magazine put it like this, '*In 1776 England lost her Colonies. The Beatles, last week, took them back*'.

I was heavily influenced by The Rolling Stones, as much for their looks and style, as their music. The Stones' music was distinctive, a mixture of Rock and rough 1950s Rhythm & Blues, with the harmonica and bluesy base guitar, influenced by American blues singers, such as Muddy Waters and Chuck Berry. The Stones were known for their wild rock star personalities and became one of the few rock bands that became a worthy rival for The Beatles. For me, back then, The Beatles and their music were for girls.

Sadly, I lost some of my affection for the Stones in the seventies, when their rhythm & blues sound was slowly replaced by modern rock music, and after Brian Jones, the founder and the original leader of the Rolling Stones, mysteriously drowned in a swimming pool accident, just weeks after being pushed out of the band. Jones was very influential, highly intelligent and a multi-instrumentalist. He formed and named the band, chose the members and the music they played, but sadly wasted it, when he developed a serious drugs problem and blew it all away. They say that by 1966, Jones was becoming obsessed with fame and attention, and that on tour he was drinking as much as one and a half litres of whiskey a day and popping pills by the handful. After his death, some said that Jones was unable to continue without his music and being part of the Rolling Stones.

A small point to mention, Jimi Hendrix dedicated a song to Brian on US television, and Jim Morrison, of the Doors, published a poem for him. Hendrix and Morrison both died within the following two years, both aged twenty-seven, the same age as Jones. Seemingly a disproportionate number of celebrated musicians have died at the age of twenty-seven, which also included, amongst a number of others, Janis Joplin, Kurt Cobain and Amy Winehouse.

Mick Jagger, the lead singer with the Rolling Stones, was my hero when I was at school, and remains so until this day. He was honoured with a knighthood, for services to popular music, in the Queen's 2002 Birthday honours. He once stated that he did not intend to be still singing '*I Can't Get No Satisfaction*' at the age of thirty. Sir Mick is now well into his seventies, and together with the band, is still singing Satisfaction, and selling out venues worldwide, more than five decades later. You would think, that after so much time, Jagger is tired of performing at least one of the Stones' major hits, but he says that he really isn't! He calls them his 'children', and still loves performing them.

One cannot mention the Rolling Stones without mentioning Keith Richards, a former choirboy and original member of the band. To some, he's an outlaw, to others, a rock god, the epiphany of the modern-day rock guitarist, an image he has maintained to this day, a likeable rogue, but a perfect example of class and quality. Guitar players in almost every rock band in the world have been influenced by Keith Richards, but the only thing that matters to him is the music. He once quoted, "*I thought rock and roll was an unassailable outlet for some pure and natural expression of rebellion. It used to be the one channel you could take, without ever having to kiss ass.*" And all this from someone who confesses to wanting to have been a librarian. Richards should not be alive at all today, given decades of drug and alcohol abuse. He eventually quit his cocaine habit, following an accident in 2006, after falling out of a tree and requiring brain surgery, resulting in a metal plate inserted in his head. He lives a far quieter life now that he is in his seventies, but says he'd hate to go around thinking of health and shit like that, and says he is still partial to beginning his day by smoking a joint! Someone once said, "*If there was ever a nuclear holocaust, only two things would survive, cockroaches and Keith Richards.*"

With the launching of Pirate Radio around the UK, during 1964, we also got to listen to music from America. Radio Caroline began broadcasting from a former Danish ferry that was renamed 'Caroline', which floated three miles of the east coast of England. Pirate Radio, in the UK, first became widespread in the early 1960s, when pop and rock music stations, such as Radio Caroline and Radio London, started to broadcast on mediumwave to the UK, from offshore ships or disused sea forts. At the time, these stations were not illegal, because they were broadcasting from international waters. The stations were set up by entrepreneurs and music enthusiasts to meet the growing demand for pop and rock music, which was not catered for by the legal BBC Radio and local services. By 1965, pirate radio had a British audience of 10 to 15 million, and by 1966, sold almost £2 million worth of advertising a year.

What was great about the pirate stations was that they played the whole of the records, as against, Radio Luxemburg, the '*Station of the Stars*', and its boring presenter, Horace Bachelor, that, for some reason, didn't. Although, they did play the British top twenty, which I would listen to, in bed on Sunday evenings. The frequency, at times, was bad, and would tend to fade away, especially when a favourite record was playing. Radio Luxemburg, for a while, was the only other option to listen to the latest bands and the type of music we wanted to hear. This was about the time I heard the phrase DJ (Disc Jockey) for the first time. The DJs, on the Pirate Stations, were young, enthusiastic and very sixties oriented. Sadly, at 3pm on August 14th, 1967, the Marine Broadcasting Offences Act brought Pirate Radio to an end.

The Americans appeared to have better solo singers, whilst the British had better bands. Popular music in the USA was tied into causes influenced by the public unrest, cultural and political differences of that period, such as the Civil Rights Movement, Flower Power, the escalation of the Vietnam War, and the assassinations of President John Kennedy and Martin Luther King.

The sixties began with a fusion of R & B with blues, called soul, music prominently African American, which gained popularity through singers such as Sam Cooke, Ray Charles, James Brown and Otis Reading. Then Motown, a Detroit-based record label, became the first African American company to reach worldwide acclaim. Tamla Motown was the heartbeat of American music, and made its mark, not just in the music industry, but society at large, with a sound that has become one of the most musical accomplishments of the 20th century. The sounds of Diana Ross and the Supremes,

Smokey Robinson, Marvin Gaye, Gladys Knight, Steve Wonder, and more, brought together a racially divided country, and touched the hearts of young and old in all parts of the world.

To this day, I still listen to the music of Sam Cooke. Sam Cooke was a very influential American songwriter, singer and civil rights activist. Cooke, with his music and incredible smooth effortless singing voice, came to be known as the inventor of soul music. His songs, such as, '*You Send Me'*, '*Wonderful World*', '*Bring it on Home to Me*', are timeless. Many successful soul artists, such as Aretha Franklin, Marvin Gaye and Al Green, contribute their rise to the influence of Cooke, and his music. Just as many great soul singers, he began his singing career singing gospel music as a child in the church. At the age of 33, Cooke was shot and killed by the manager of a motel in Los Angeles, California, on 11th December 1964. After an inquest, the courts ruled Cooke's death to be a justifiable homicide, however, since that time, the strange circumstances surrounding his death have been called into question by Cooke's family and friends. Some people have speculated that Cooke's manager, Allen Klein, might have had a role in his death. Klein owned Tracey, Ltd, which ultimately owned all rights to Cooke's recordings!

Sadly, Marvin Gaye's career ended in similar fashion. Gaye, during the sixties and seventies, had a successful career as singer, songwriter and record producer, recording unforgettable songs, such as, '*I Heard it Through the Grapevine*', '*How Sweet It Is (To Be Loved By You)*', helping to shape the sound of Motown, and later, the classic, '*Sexual Healing*'. On 1st April 1984, after intervening in a fight between his parents, his father, Marvin Gaye Sr, entered Gaye's bedroom and shot him twice, with a shot in the heart proving fatal.

Then, there was the infectious surf music, reflecting the laid-back life style of spoiled Californian kids and surfers. The best know band for this type of music was The Beach Boys, with songs like '*Good Vibrations*' and, '*Wouldn't It Be Nice*'.

The Band was co-founded by Brian Wilson, who explored with an unorthodox approach to recording techniques, he wrote and produced a string of hit singles, and was the creative force in establishing the '*California Sound*', representing the youth culture of that time. Wilson, in spite of his lifelong struggle with drug abuse and mental illness, is considered as a genius. At what was the peak of his career, he went into seclusion, and only revived his career years later, when it was discovered that his psychologist had been exerting an excessive amount of control over his life and finances. The band's album, '*Pet Sounds*', released during 1966, was placed by Rolling Stone at Number 2 on their list of the 500 greatest albums of all time. Paul McCartney cited the song, '*God Only Knows*', as one of the most beautiful songs ever written, and the album influenced The Beatles when producing their 1967 album, '*Sgt Pepper's Hearts Club Band*'.

In contrast, The Doors were unique and one of the most controversial and influential American rock acts of the 1960s, in no small way, because of the magnetic personality and extraordinary lyrics coming from the lead singer, songwriter and poet, Jim Morrison. There has never been another band quite like The Doors, and over fifty years later, their music and legacy are more influential than ever. The music they produced had extraordinary power. Whilst other bands were singing about love, peace and happiness, The Doors, with their combination of keyboard complexities, infused with dynamic drum and guitar expressions and poetic sometimes-dark lyrics, describing sex and death, went where no band had been before.

The Doors' career, however, was short lived. Formed in 1965, they shot to fame in 1967, with their first hit '*Light My Fire*', but the band disbanded in 1973, following the untimely death of Jim Morrison in Paris, a couple of years previous, during July 1971, when Patricia, his common law wife, discovered him at their apartment dead in his bathtub. The cause of Morrison's death remains unknown, as an autopsy was never performed, it was determined to be a heart attack, linked to a dependency that he developed, over the years, for alcohol. He was laid to rest at the Pere Lachaise Cemetery, in Paris, reputed to be the most visited cemetery in the world, where amongst the 800,000 souls, lay the tombs of Chopin, Edith Piaf, Rossini and Oscar Wild. After Morrison's death, the movies, documentaries, books, and relaunching of the Doors music, their popularity resurged. Fans from all over the world began to visit Jim's gravestone, and for a while, the cemetery became the third most popular tourist attraction in Paris, after the Eiffel Tower and the Louvre.

It's interesting that in one of his many quotes, he said, "*People fear death even more than pain. It's strange they fear death. Life hurts a lot more than death. At the point of death, the pain is over. Yeah, I guess it's a friend.*"

To this day, Morrison is considered as one of the most iconic and influential frontmen in rock band history, representing the generation gap and a youth rebellious counterculture of his era. During a 1967 concert in New Haven, Connecticut, Morrison became the first rock artist to be arrested onstage, during a concert performance, following a local cop catching him having sex with a girl in a shower backstage, prior to the start of the show. Unaware that Morrison was the lead singer in the band, he ordered them to leave. The girl disappeared, but Morrison gave the cop some lip, before taking to the stage, only to be dragged off the stage by police, after him inventing a song about his experience with 'the little men in blue', and what had taken place earlier backstage. He was taken to the local police station and charged with inciting a riot, indecency and obscenity.

Even though The Doors' active career ended in 1973, they remain one of the most popular bands of all time, having sold over 33 million records in the USA and over 100 million records worldwide.

If you have never listened to The Doors, then you should. After the first hit '*Light My Fire*', came some unique pieces of music, such as '*Riders on the Storm*', '*Break on Through (To the Other Side)*', '*Hello I Love You*', and '*The End*', featured in the movie about the Vietnam War, '*Apocalypse Now*'.

Flower Power, preaching peace and harmony, came about through an American sixties' movement. These were Hippies that had a vocal opposition to the United States' involvement in the Vietnam War, and proclaimed that we all should "Make love, not war". Their spiritual home was San Francisco, and much of their music was fuelled by psychedelic and mind-altering drug use. The baby boom, following the war, was now in its teen years, a large force of well-to-do middle-class Americans, many in their high school and college years, who rejected conformity, and following in the footsteps of their parents. They rejected established organisations, criticised the upper classes, and were against nuclear weapons and war.

The Hippies would preach peace and to, "Love your neighbour," and hand flowers in the streets to passers-by, with the summer of 1967 becoming known as the Summer of Love, the hit song, '*San Francisco (Be Sure to Wear [Some] Flowers in Your Hair)*', by Scott McKenzie, became the Hippies' national anthem.

Flower Power clothing was loose-fitting, free and easy, frayed bell-bottomed jeans, sandals or moccasins, headbands and love beads.

It did not take long for the Flower Power revolution to cross the Atlantic to Britain, although in a more moderate form. A sign that times were changing socially, was when, in the summer of 1967, The Duke of Bedford welcomed music fans and Hippies, by giving permission to hold a rock concert in the beautiful stately grounds of Woburn Abbey. The festival, billed as a '*Festival of the Flower Children*', a non-stop 3-day happening, featured leading bands, including The Small Faces, The Bee Gees. Jeff Beck, Eric Burdon, to name a few.

Just as I turned up to meet my friends, dressed as a mod, a couple of years earlier, one of our crowd turned up one evening as a hippie. He was dressed in a denim cap, loose fitting cotton shirt, baggy linen trousers, sandals and a guitar slung over his shoulder, which he couldn't play, he could only strum a few cords. Now it was my turn, he looked a twat. He brought with him his new hippie girlfriend, wearing what could have been her grandmother's dress and cardigan, no bra (a sign of the counter culture of the time) and a wide brimmed hat, with flowers pinned around it. He introduced her and said her name was '*Dog*', to a subdued response from the lads, before saying hi. Her response was putting two fingers in the air, saying, "Peace!" She immediately got a new name from us, it was Jugs or Jug'sy, because of her big boobs.

The climax of the hippie culture was probably Woodstock, during August 1969, where a rock concert for 50,000 was organised. However, it got out of control, when, as many as 500,000 people descended on Bethel Dairy Farm NY for the Woodstock Music & Art Festival (most without tickets). For four days, they camped out in the mud and the rain. to take part in what was described as a peaceful happening and the icon of the 1960s hippie counterculture. Legendary acts, such as The Who, Janis Joblin, Joe Cocker, Jimi Hendrix, Creedence Clearwater Revival, were amongst the thirty or so bands and celebrities that performed.

It was around this time that the Hippie Movement, for a number of reasons, began its decline. Maybe it was that these kids were just growing up, or the subsequent rock festivals were becoming drug infested and violent and were no longer the peaceful environment that they preached.

An example of this would be the December 1969 free Altamont Music Festival, organised by the Rolling Stones, to conclude their US tour. The festival was held at the Altamont Speedway Stadium, in Northern California. The concert, which was supposed to be California's answer to the New York Woodstock festival, had already been rejected at an alternative venue by San Francisco officials due to the lack of crowd control precautions.

Approximately 300,000 people attended the concert, which featured Santana, Jefferson Airplane, The Flying Burrito Brothers, and Crosby, Stills, Nash & Young, with The Rolling Stones being the final act. Security was provided by the Hells Angels motorcycle gang, who were provided with all the free beer they wanted for their efforts. (Who could not accept such an offer?). The rock band, 'Grateful Dead', were also on the bill, but dropped out for their own safety, when they heard that Jefferson Airplane singer, Marty Balin, had been knocked unconscious by one of the Hells Angels during a scuffle, whilst he was performing. The Hells Angels were hired on the suggestion of the Grateful Dead. It became obvious from the very start that neither the artists nor the festivalgoers were comfortable with the gang's presence

Things got out of hand during the Rolling Stones final act, and Jagger pleaded with the crowd to stay cool. The Stones, themselves, were becoming concerned for their own security. The main incident was when an 18-year-old guy named Meredith Hunter approached the stage and climbed a speaker, to get a better view of the band, but got into an affray with an Angel, who tried to drag him off. He ran away, with some Angels following him through the crowd. Hunter pulled a gun and pointed it at an Angel and in the direction of the stage, but it was too late, some Angels surrounded him, and he was stabbed twice, dragged away, beaten and stabbed some more. Efforts at a nearby medical tent to save him were futile. It all happened just twenty feet from the stage, where Jagger was performing '*Under My Thumb*'.

Sadly, the Altamont Speedway Free Festival is best remembered for the considerable violence, including the stabbing and death of Meredith Hunter, and three accidental deaths, two caused by a hit-and-run car accident, and one by LSD-induced drowning in an irrigation canal. Scores were injured, numerous cars were stolen and then abandoned, and there was extensive property damage.

But, the *Sharon Tate Murders*, just a few days before the Woodstock Festival, certainly left its mark on this free-loving generation of Hippies.

The Sharon Tate Murders are probably the most grotesque, unaccountable, gruesome murders carried out against a well-known celebrity ever. Sharon, almost nine months pregnant, the twenty-six-year-old wife of film director Roman Polanski, and four of her houseguests were tortured, stabbed and shot to death, when hippie cult leader Charles Manson and four of his followers (The Manson Family) broke into their home on the outskirts of Los Angeles. The next evening, further murders took place when a businessman and his wife were brutally killed at their home. In all, there were nine murders at four locations, leaving Hollywood in a state of panic.

Manson and three of his followers, Susan Atkins, Patricia Krenwinkel and Leslie Van Houten were arrested, charged and put on trial during June, the following year. Tex Watson, Manson's right-hand man and principle killer in the murders, was tried separately.

The trial horrified the nation, when, during the hearings, those that carried out the murders turned it into a circus, with outrageous outbursts or singing, smiling and chatting, showing no remorse for their actions or concern to the proceedings. Grim details emerged at the trial of how each participated in the murders. Atkins admitted to holding Tate down, whilst Watson stabbed her multiple times, whilst she was begging not to harm her unborn child, she also admitted to writing the word '*Pig*', using Tate's blood, and messages using her victim's blood on the walls. She was a former church choirgirl!

Manson planned, instigated and ordered the killings, but didn't participate himself. He was convicted and given the death sentence, which was changed to a life sentence, when during 1972, the California Supreme Court declared the death penalty as unconstitutional. He died on 19th November 2017, at the age of eighty-three, in the hospital of a Californian prison, of natural causes. An interesting note is that the Beach Boys released a song written by Charles Manson, '*Cease to Exist*', on their 1969 album *20/20*!

There was also the anti-war movement and protest songs. As a young man who had recently left school and started work, I was intrigued with Bob Dylan and his songs against the establishment. His songs became anthems for social unrest. The lyrics, his gravelly voice and the sound of the harmonica, supporting an acoustic guitar, to me, sounded unique.

I was very happy at that age and had nothing to be rebellious about, but somehow our generation were very opinionated and felt we needed to question everything. Dylan's songs, such as, '*Blowing in the Wind*' and, '*The Times They Are A-Changing*', with such lyrics as ...*Come senators and congressmen, please heed the call, don't stand in the doorway, don't block up the hall, for he that gets hurt will be he who has stalled, there's a battle outside raging, it'll soon shake your windows and rattle your walls, for the times they are a-changing...* His music, lyrically, spoke much louder than The Beatles and the Rolling Stones. While others were singing about having fun, girls and heartbreak, Dylan was singing about government oppression, racism, changing society, which had journalists suggesting that he was a spokesman for our generation.

At the time of writing, it was announced that Bob Dylan has been awarded The Noble Prize for Literature, the first time ever awarded to a singer. Controversially, he did not attend to receive the award at the Noble Banquet in Stockholm, on 10th December 2016. His speech was given to the United States Ambassador to Sweden for presentation on his behalf.

The youngest person to win the Nobel Peace Prize and also associated with the protests of the sixties, was Dr Martin Luther King Jr, in 1964, at the age of thirty-five years. Dr King was the leader of the modern American Civil Rights Movement, and spoke out strongly against the Vietnam War, and about international peace. His nonviolent leadership and powerful speeches, against segregation and for racial equality, inspired a younger generation of Americans and Anti-War Protesters, much of which is conveyed in the folk music of that era. King's '*I Have a Dream*' speech, during the organised 'March to Washington for Jobs and Freedom' August 1963, is regarded as one of the finest speeches in the history of America. An estimated 250,000 people attended the march and was the largest gathering for civil rights of its time.

Martin Luther King was shot and assassinated 04 April 1968, whilst standing on the balcony of a motel in Memphis, Tennessee. He was 39 years of age.

Musicians of all kinds protested through their music, and to this day if you listen to the songs, they describe and express the feelings and emotions of that period in time. Check some out: *Bring Them Home and Where Have all the Flowers Gone?,* Pete Seeger; *Give Peace a Chance,* John Lennon; *People Have the Power,* Patti Smith; *If I had a Hammer,* Peter Paul and Mary; *War*, Edwin Star; *A Change is Gonna Come,* Sam Cook; *Alabama,* John Coltrane; *With God on Our Side,* Bob Dylan.

The anti-war movement continued to grow to the extent that decorated Vietnam War heroes began to march side by side with the demonstrators, and a number of them discarding their war medals by throwing them into the Whitehouse grounds.

Widely recognised as one of the most creative and influential musicians of the 20th century is Jimi Hendrix. I remember being completely blown away when I first watched him perform his first successful hit single, '*Hey Joe*', on a Television show, sometime during 1967. His rise to international fame took place in just four short years, after being discovered performing in a small club in Greenwich Village New York, by the Animals base guitarist Chas Chandler. Chandler was so impressed with Jimmy's performance; he returned some months later to sign Hendrix to an agreement that would have him move to London to form a new band.

Desperate to follow in the footsteps of his own British guitar idols, Jimi touched down on British soil on Saturday 24th September 1966. It is said that he arrived at Heathrow airport, carrying a small bag with his guitar, a change of clothes, pink plastic hair curlers, and a jar of cream for his acne. Accompanying him was Chas Chandler, with whom Jimi had agreed to follow to England, only if he promised to introduce him to his icon Eric Clapton, who was, at that time, with Cream. Within forty-eight hours, he would take to the stage for an unprecedented onstage jam with Clapton, Ginger Baker and Jack Bruce.

Hendrix was an entirely self-taught musician, and his inability to read music made him concentrate even harder on the music he heard, which probably resulted in his innovative style of combining a controlled distorted fuzzy feedback original musical sound. He embraced the influences of blues, ballads, rock, R&B, and jazz, a collection of styles that continue to make Hendrix one of the most popular figures in the history of rock music.

He performed with outrageous guitar techniques, such as playing with his teeth or with the guitar behind his back, with sounds emerging long after touching the strings, amazing his audiences, and contributing to his reputation as a showman. A more subtle unorthodox technique of his, however, was that he played a right-handed guitar with his left hand, which meant the strings were upside down.

One of Jimi's greatest performances was probably in 1969, at Woodstock. He started his performance by ignoring concerns from the organisers that he might spark a riot by playing the USA National Anthem, given that, to some, at that time, it was not a symbol of national pride because of America's continued occupation of Vietnam. However, he could not see a greater stage to display his disgust and contempt about the war, and his performance that day has become an integral part of American history.

Jimi Hendrix died in London, on September 18th, 1970. The circumstances surrounding his death remain rather mysterious, and how he passed away is still a matter of debate. The post-mortem revealed that he had vomited in his sleep and choked to death having overdosed on red wine and sleeping tablets, in search of a full night's sleep He was described as a tortured soul and a long-time recreational drug user. Those who knew him well, have come up with dozens of explanations as to what happened that night. Accident, suicide or murder. How did Jimi Hendrix die? Perhaps we will never know.

During the sixties, the major rock bands and performers would go on the road and turn up at the most unlikely places to perform shows. The venues were not planned months ahead, as they are today in enormous stadiums and purposely built arenas. Small venues with screaming fans have been replaced by huge arenas that offer a more commercialised experience. Rock bands would play anywhere they could, such as theatres, small night clubs, town halls, and pubs, probably at the mercy of, and arranged at short notice by, their promotors and managers. I saw Chris Farlowe (his hit, '*Out of Time*', was number one the day England won the World Cup) perform at the height of his career in the assembly room of The Coventry Arms pub, the Yardbirds' guitarist Jeff Beck, and his band in the Matrix Factory workers' canteen hall.

I do remember that we would never pay the admission at the door, of night clubs, before doing a commando type evaluation of the premises for other ways to enter. This included climbing and looking over walls and in windows, checking access through adjoining buildings and locations of toilets, fire and exit doors. One of lads would then pay to go in, and check from the inside, and later take a pass to come out, and give us a plan of which windows and doors etc. could be opened from the inside how many bouncers (security) were around, and where they were posted. It was a bit of a cat-and-mouse game, but I think the bouncers secretly enjoyed the challenge, and the opportunity to catch some kid trying to get in without paying, rough him up a bit, and kick him out by the scruff of the neck, whereas we would enjoy bragging about beating the system.

The Locarno Ballroom, sometimes referred to as the Rock House, is arguably as important as any venue Coventry has ever had. I remember that it had a revolving stage so the band could hand over to the following group without the music stopping. Over the years, the list of live acts that appeared there, visiting the city, quite simply reads like a who's who of British popular music. I saw many perform there, such as Ike and Tina Turner, The Who, The Small Faces, Georgie Fame and The Blue Flames, The Troggs, to name a few. It was also the venue where Chuck Berry recorded his number one hit, '*My Ding A Ling*', in 1972. A Led Zeppelin gig there, was interrupted by a bomb scare. Apparently, the only person who refused to leave the venue was Robert Plant, but they did resume and finish the gig. In spite of the popularity of the performers, the attendances compared with today were often small in numbers, probably because of the short notice that the gigs were arranged, and again the fact that social media, google and the apps promoting entertainment were not around until years later.

I remember vividly, sometime in 1967, at seventeen years of age, watching 'The Who' perform at the Coventry Locarno. They were introduced by the local DJ, appearing by way of the revolving stage, singing their first ever hit, '*I Can't Explain*', and going on to perform one of the most exciting shows I ever saw. Keith Moon performed a drum solo that would have to be seen to be believed. The Who was different, their attitude, their style, their music, and aggression made them revolutionaries in rock music (which has become timeless). *Ask my American friend who I referred to at the beginning of this story!* During the mid to late sixties, during the mod era, I believe, whether we knew it or not, we were probably influenced by The Who and their music more than The Beatles, The Rolling Stones or any of the other great bands at that time. The Who were mods, and captured the youthful rebellion, and that's where we wanted to be.

After their first single release in 1964, '*I Can't Explain*', they rolled out hits, such as '*My Generation*', '*The Kids Are Alright*', '*Substitute*', '*Pictures of Lilly*', '*I Can See for Miles and Miles*', '*I'm a Boy*', and '*Happy Jack*'. They blew away the crowds with their performances at the major rock concerts, including Woodstock, where it was considered to be one of the finest performances of the Woodstock concert, and sealed their reputation as one of the world's most exciting rock bands, however, Pete Townshend said afterwards that he thought The Who's performance, "*Was fucking awful.*"

All the band members were individually extremely talented, with Pete Townshend being considered one of the greatest guitarists and composers in the world of rock. The climax of his performances on stage was to smash his guitar into pieces. John Entwistle was once voted by Rolling Stone Magazine as the best bass guitar player in the world. Entwistle passed away in the Hard Rock Hotel, Las Vegas, on 27 June 2002, aged fifty-seven. One newspaper reported his death by saying, "The bass player from The Who, died in a fashion any self-respecting rock legend would be proud of." After a concert and some drinks in the bar, he went to bed with a stripper, but never woke up. The cause was later reported, that his death was due to him having taken cocaine with a pre-existing heart condition. Roger Daltrey, founder and lead singer with a unique voice and charismatic stage performances – his talents contributed to the group's sense of showmanship. Keith Moon, rated by Rolling Stone Magazine as the number two greatest drummer in the world, between number one, Ginger Baker, of the band Cream, and number three, John Bonham, of Led Zeppelin. Before Moon's time, drums were just a simple way of keeping the beat. I don't think I ever took any interest in drummers until I saw Moon on stage; he played the drums as if they were the lead instrument, at the same time spinning and juggling the sticks. Keith died in London, on 7 September 1978, at the age of thirty-two, from an accidental drug overdose of the prescription drug Heminevrin, normally prescribed to combat alcoholism. The list of The Who's incredible talents goes on and on, from their performances, their individuality and music, that stretches from basic rock to masterpieces of theatrical rock operas, such as *Quadrophenia* and *Tommy*.

The band were also notorious for wrecking luxury hotel rooms and blowing up toilets when they were on tour, causing thousands of pounds of damage. Keith Moon became known as the worst hotel guest ever, and the band were infamously barred from the Holiday Inn, Sheraton and Hilton Hotel chains. There is a story of Moon, celebrating his 21st birthday driving his car into the hotel pool, blowing up a toilet and starting a cake fight. Another, which I am not sure if true, he drove his car through the glass doors of a luxury hotel and across to the reception, got out and casually asked for room availability. Moon made the Punk Bands of the seventies and your Ozzy Osborn's and Marilyn Manson's look like well-behaved schoolboys. Roger Daltrey described Keith Moon as living his entire life as a fantasy.

The Who, in spite of the large number of hit records they produced, never had a number one record in the British charts. However, Pete Townshend did. In 1969, Townshend created a band of ex associates that performed songs, written by himself and the other band members. The band, 'Thunderclap Newman', had a single that hit number one called '*Something in the Air*', and to this day appears in television commercials, film soundtracks and compilations

One evening, I went to visit a friend, when his elder sister appeared with two tickets to see Otis Redding and asked me if I wanted to go with her. Well I did. We had no money for the train, so hitch-hiked from Coventry to Birmingham. It was 02 April 1967, '*The Otis Redding Show*' at the Birmingham Theatre. His supporting acts were Sam and Dave *Hold on I'm a Coming*; Arthur Conley *Sweet Soul Music*; Eddie Floyd *Knock on Wood;* backed by Booker T. and the M.G. *Green Onions*. And that's how it was, from one moment to the next, we were watching one of the top Soul and R & B shows and its performers of the decade.

Otis Redding died later that year, in December, when the plane he was travelling on, between shows in the USA, hit bad weather and crashed into Lake Monona, a few minutes before landing near Madison. A song he wrote just three days before his death, '*(Sitting On) The Dock of the Bay*', became the biggest posthumous hit of all time, both in the USA and Great Britain.

There is one performer I was lucky enough to see twice, during his visits to the U.K. and Coventry, someone who impressed me and entertained like no other. He is considered the pioneer of rock and roll, the first wild man of rock and roll, the king of rock and roll, he was given the nickname 'The Killer'. He was born in Louisiana, to a very poor but religious farming family, and started playing the piano at the age of nine. He was kicked out of school at an early age, and his mother enrolled him in a local bible institute so he could sing and play evangelical songs which he did, until one day at the age of twelve, he played in church assembly a boogie-woogie version of the hymn, '*My God is Real*', which ended his association with the church institute that very same day.

Jerry Lee Lewis is widely hailed as one of the most influential pianists in the history of rock and roll. In an often-quoted tribute, Elvis Presley once said that if he could play the piano like Lewis, he would quit singing. Lewis's pivotal role in popularising the piano in rock and roll is indisputable. Up until his arrival, the music had been primarily associated with guitars. Depending on his audience, he could play and sing anything from gospel, country and western, jazz, rhythm and blues, to rock and roll. He could have them in tears singing *Danny Boy, The Green Green Grass of Home*, before bursting into *Great Balls of Fire or Whole Lotta Shaking Going On*. Lewis was an incendiary showman, who often played the piano standing up, with his fists, elbows, feet, and backside, sometimes climbing on top of the piano during gigs, and occasionally setting one on fire.

Many believe that Jerry Lee would have been bigger than Elvis Presley if his personal life had not preceded him. At 16 he fell in love with a preacher's daughter, recalling, "*She set my world afire, but she would not have sex before marriage, so I married her*." But it took him about 30 minutes to figure out he had made a mistake, that he had married too young. He married his pregnant second wife two weeks before divorcing his first. It was a volatile marriage, and he filed for divorce weeks after their second child was born. But it was his third marriage that landed him in deep trouble.

His career plummeted after it became known that at twenty-two, he had married his third wife, who was his thirteen-year-old cousin. On his arrival in England to perform a number of shows, someone asked this young girl who was with the group, who she was. She innocently replied, "I am Jerry's wife," and the press immediately jumped on the story. He was labelled a baby snatcher and boycotted by record companies and fans. His earnings of US$ 10,000 for a performance dropped to as low as US$ 250, but he carried on performing and gradually made a comeback. The marriage lasted thirteen years and was probably the only real love of his life. But she caught him cheating. He married four more times, his fourth wife drowned in a swimming pool whilst visiting a friend, and his fifth died at home under mysterious circumstances. Altogether, Jerry had six children, four sons and two daughters. Again, sadly, one of his sons drowned in a swimming pool at a very young age, and another in an accident when he overturned the jeep he was driving. He once remarked, "*Seemed like I was always on my way to the graveyard, at one time it seemed like I was burying somebody every week. If it wasn't my mama, it was my boys…A steady stream.*"

A lot of the time, Lewis liked living dangerously, surrounded by guns and fast cars, he flipped ten Cadillacs in one reckless year and destroyed another two Rolls-Royces. There is also a story of the time that a drunken Jerry Lee pulled his car up against the front gates of Graceland at three in the morning and demanded to see Elvis but was told that Elvis didn't want to be disturbed. Waving a gun towards the house, Jerry shouted, "Who the hell does that son of a bitch think he is? Doesn't wanna be disturbed!" The gate security guard called the police, who arrived, cuffed him and took him away.

Jerry Lee was inducted into the Rock & Roll Hall of Fame in 1986, and continued to put on brilliant shows well into his 70s. Today, Jerry says he spends a lot of time worried as to whether, when he dies, he will go to hell or heaven. He thinks it was not the music itself, but the lifestyle that was un-godly, but he says he did the best he could.

Sometimes, we would go, and watch bands perform at the Warwick University, on the outskirts of Coventry.

The bands that played at the universities were somewhat diverse from the run-of-the-mill bands, just as were the university students themselves. They tended to favour the folk rock and psychedelic type, and performers like 'Crosby Stills and Nash', 'Deep Purple', 'John Mayall and The Blues Breakers', and what about the 'Bonzo Dog Doo-Dah Band', which was formed by a group of art students, best known for their hit record 'I'm the Urban Spaceman'. We always felt, with the university students, when we went to these gigs, that they held an air of superiority and had a way of talking down to outsiders. One time, we were there to watch, I think, 'The Crazy World of Arthur Brown', when I got chatting with a plain-Jane type student. I felt confident with my fresh haircut, light grey check suit with side vents, white shirt with stiff cutback detachable collar, slim knitted tie and Hush Puppies. She said her name was Sophia and came from Kent. I tried to act interested and intelligent by asking her what she was studying, until the conversation went pare shaped.

"I am in my second year, studying anthropology."

"Hmm, that's interesting. Is it about ants?"

A smile. "No, it's human biology and physiological characteristics, and their evolution."

Me thinking, *what language do they speak in Kent, or have I had too much beer? Best change the subject.*

"So, how are you enjoying the band?"

"I am not enjoying it; I don't like this band at all."

"Then, who are you into?"

"Well, I like Jefferson Airplane and Paul Butterfield."

Who the fuck are they, I think to myself, *this is getting awkward, until she asks me,*

"So, what are you studying here?"

Proudly, I told her, "I am not at the university. I work in a car factory as an apprentice toolmaker."

She stood back, her face had a look of shock, she looked me up and down, as if I had just crawled out of the toilet. "Oh, you are a factory worker," she turned her back on me, and continued talking to her friends as if I was not there.

I could never understand why university students acted so sophisticated and thought they were so superior to others. They hung around the universities, ignorantly believing that knowledge is certain just because they heard it from their professors and read it in their textbooks. Only a limited number learn for themselves by research and making their own judgments and come to think like expert scientists and engineers. An apprenticeship lasted for five years whereby over that time, we were assessed for our time keeping, attendance, exam results, our ability to conduct the work we were given and progress reports from the various heads of departments, where we had been assigned.

The essence of knowledge is having the ability to apply it.

Arthur Brown, by the way, was a crazy performer who quickly earned a reputation for both his powerful voice and his outlandish performances, including entering on stage wearing a burning metal helmet, which led to occasional mishaps. During an early appearance at the Windsor Festival, in 1967, Brown wore a kind of bowl on his head soaked in methanol. The fuel poured over his head by accident and caught fire, two bystanders doused the flames by pouring beer on his head, preventing any serious injury. The flaming head then became an Arthur Brown signature. On occasions, he also stripped naked while performing, most notably in Italy, where, after setting his hair on fire, he was arrested and deported. He was also notable for the extreme make-up he wore onstage, which would later be reflected in the stage acts of Kiss, Alice Cooper and Marilyn Manson. The song that made him famous was '*Fire*', which went on to sell over one million copies.

Another likably rogue that I remember from around that time, is the 'longest-serving leader of a political party in the UK'. It was a mid-week gig, in a small nightclub, in the centre of Coventry. The lights were dimmed, and he was carried to the stage in ceremonial fashion, inside a coffin, to the sound of the death march. The coffin bearers were the club's bouncers (today called security). He had a number of songs that made the charts, including, '*Jack the Ripper*' and '*Dracula's Daughter*'. David Edward Sutch, also known as 3rd Earl of Harrow, or simply 'Screaming Lord Sutch', was an English musician and the founder of the official 'Monster Raving Loony Party', which he launched in 1963. He stood in numerous parliamentary elections and holds the record for losing more than forty elections. Sadly, he had a history of depression, and committed suicide by hanging on 16 June 1999.

A spokesman for the prime minister at the time, said, "*Lord Sutch will be much missed. For many years, he made a unique contribution to British politics, our elections will never be quite the same without him.*" Following his death, there were calls from his party for a statue to be erected to Lord Sutch, outside the Houses of Parliament, next to the statue of Sir Winston Churchill, who was one of the Loony leader's heroes. One has to smile at the British tongue-in-cheek humour.

For a couple of years, between 1966 and 1968, a band, which became widely known as the world's first super group, and went on to sell 15 million records worldwide, were favourites at that time with university and upper white-collar classes that were looking for something different, were 'Cream'. The band consisted of three highly talented musicians, base/lead vocalist Jack Bruce, guitarist/vocalist Eric Clapton and drummer Ginger Baker. Their sound was a unique blend of blues, psychedelic rock and the combination of Clapton's guitar playing, the powerful voice of Jack Bruce and raging drumming of Baker, produced a style of music unmatched until this day. Their *Wheels of Fire* album became the world's first platinum-selling double album.

From the beginning, the band faced problems that led to them breaking up in November 1968. There had been continues disagreements between Bruce and Baker, and an antagonism that went back to before the band was even formed. Clapton felt that the band members were finding it difficult to agree on anything, and that the other two were showing off during gigs. He once mentioned that during one performance he stopped playing, and they didn't even notice! The three of them had named the band 'Cream' because they thought themselves to be elite, and the top players of their respective instruments, of that period. Which, maybe they were!

For those middle of the road, more serious, single, lonely, and/or university type people, that could not get their heads around the rock, blues and soul bands, there was always the folk scene. Probably the best of this kind of music, was produced by two school friends from New York, who, at a young age, learned to harmonise and write music together. Simon and Garfunkel, with what was described as their folk-rock sound, went on to be one of the biggest selling and most celebrated duos of the sixties. Their hits included, '*The Sound of Silence*', '*The Boxer*', '*Parsley, Sage, Rosemary and Thyme*', and a number one single, '*Mrs Robinson*', a song that featured in the 1967 movie, '*The Graduate*', starring Dustin Hoffman and Anne Bancroft. The music world was shocked when they announced their breakup in 1970, after the release of their most successful recording, and one of the world's best-selling compositions, '*Bridge over Troubled Water*'. Their troubled water continued over the years, and the bridge was never properly repaired, in spite of them reuniting for shows on a number of occasions, where the body language said it all. The break-up was cited as a sometimes-rocky relationship, which led to artistic disagreements, although, years later, in an interview, Simon mentioned it was because Garfunkel wanted to be more involved with movies for six months of the year, and the remaining six months, work with him. "*So that really pissed me off,*" he said. "*And, I just decided, that's the end of that. I don't want to do this anymore*."

During the same period, on our side of the pond, a Scottish singer and songwriter, with his own distinctive style of folk, rock, and later, psychedelic music became successful, following live performances on *Ready Steady Go* and popular TV shows. To begin with, the critics unkindly accused 'Donovan' of imitating Bob Dylan, which was unfair, as he generated his own blend of music and songs. He did admit, however, of being somewhat influenced by Dylan in his younger days. His early UK hits were, '*Catch the Wind*', '*Colours*', and, '*Universal Soldier*' (which became popular with the anti-war movement in the US), and in September

1966, '*Sunshine Superman*' topped the American charts for a week and got to number five in the UK.

Over a period of time, he began to lose his Dylan image, becoming accepted for his own style and blend of psychedelic Eastern tone music, probably fuelled by his cannabis, and, sometimes, LSD habit. His music and lyrics in songs, such as, '*Sunshine Superman*', '*Hurdy Gurdy Man*', and '*Epistle to Dippy*', show a drug related influence. Donovan can boast that he was the first high-profile British pop star to be arrested for possession of marijuana, during 1966.

What followed was a long series of arrests, including members of The Beatles, The Rolling Stones, and claims in the media of others, such as The Who (specifically naming Pete Townshend) and The Moody Blues throwing parties, where hallucinatory drugs and marijuana were used freely. When the police raided a party at Keith Richards home, during February 1967, it was later discovered that it was News of the World Reporters that had tipped off the police. Newspaper headlines concerning our favourite rock stars and drugs, sold papers!

And not to forget, the '*reggae music*'. During the late sixties, on Saturday nights, two or three carloads of us (excluding those that had fallen into the trap of regular girlfriends) would drive over to Birmingham for a night out. On the way, we would stop off at a couple of pubs, I think, The Swan at Yardley and The Bulls Head, just to keep our alcohol intake at a reasonable level, before paying the extortionate nightclub prices. There were a number of popular night clubs, if I remember, The Whiskey A Go and The Rum Runner, to name a couple, places where Black Sabbath and Roy Wood, of the band Wizzard, frequented and started their careers, although we would normally end up at the Locarno. The Locarno was more of a ballroom than a night club and had a dress code whereby a tie was required. Apparently, a Greek fish and chip shop, just around the corner, would sell ties if someone needed one to get in. For some reason, in some clubs, it became a trend to have UV lighting over the dance floor, which was horrendous. It would show up stains, and every speckle of dust on your clothes and in your hair, show up your freckles and the whites of your eyes. One of the lads had a couple of false dentures at the front that became blazing white when he smiled, which he refrained from doing when chatting up girls. A good-looking girl you chatted up at the bar could become vampire like, when you got her on the dance floor.

The main dance floor, bars and balconies were on the lower level, as I remember, and above, up a stairway was another dance hall, much smaller, which was frequented by the Birmingham West Indian, Caribbean crowd. It was here that I developed my love for reggae music. I don't really remember the names of the artist or the songs of that time, but I remember how much I liked the sound and the atmosphere it created. Reggae is a form of music which originated in Jamaica, combining elements of calypso and rhythm and blues, featuring many instruments, typically acoustic guitar, banjo, bongo, steel drums and keyboard. There was one very catchy song that I recall, recorded in 1968 by a Jamaican reggae singer, by the name of Max Romeo. The song was called '*Wet Dream*'. The lyrics went…

Every night me go to sleep, me have wet dream.
Lie down girl, let me push it up, push it up, lie down.
Look how you're big and fat, like Big Shot.
Give the crumpet to Big Shot
Give the Fanny to me.
Lie down girl, let me push it up, push it up,

Such a catchy tune, I can't think why it was never aired on the BBC Radio!

It was the late Desmond Dekker who pioneered the sounds of Jamaican reggae into Britain. It was his 1969 hit, '*Israelites*', which, according to many, quickly established the British reggae genre. In April 1969, 'The Israelites' was the first ever reggae song to top the UK Singles Chart, making Dekker Jamaica's first international reggae superstar. In the wake of his success in the 1970s, came a host of others.

In 1973, a teenage Rastafarian young boy, from the depths of Trench town, named Robert Nesta Marley, and his band The Wailers, took reggae music to another height and widened reggae music to a worldwide audience. To this day, the late Bob Marley's song, '*One Love*', is in my top ten of all-time favourites. His band, with one of the original members, are still touring. I watched them at the Irish Village Dubai in 2016. The show was a sell-out, to an audience of young and old, of many nationalities, who all knew the words to the music, including a couple of local Arab ladies, dressed in abayas, that were not shy to join in. Bob Marley died at the age of thirty-six, of melanoma, on 11th May 1981, and left us with an immeasurable collection of mesmerising hits, which will forever gratify the hearts and minds for generations to come. His last words to his son were, "*Money can't buy life.*"

Our visits to Birmingham would conclude at 02.00 am on the Sunday morning, when the nightclub doors were closed. A crowd of us would kick a football around in an empty multi-storey carpark for a while, before heading back to Coventry (a football was always kept ready in the cars), but not before stopping at a Pakistani takeaway along the Coventry Road. What better way to finish up a night out, after six or seven pints of lager, than a tray of chips swimming in curry sauce.

Not only did our visits to Birmingham introduce us to reggae music but also curry. Since that time, Birmingham has become known as the curry capital of the UK, with a wide selection of curry houses spread across the city. But where did this love affair between Brum and curry come from? *Balti* houses began popping up in the Midlands city in the late 60s to early 70s, and due to their popularity amongst locals, they've been growing ever since. The Balti dish was created by the local Pakistani/Kashmiri community that decided to bring a taste of their home cooking to the streets of Birmingham, by blending various herbs and spices to create the perfect dish that could also be enjoyed by the Western locals. A true Birmingham Balti must be served in the same thin steel bowl it is cooked in over a hot flame, as it is this 'balti' bowl that gives the dish its name.

Chapter 12
Entertainment

I got rabies shots for biting the head off a bat, but that's okay. The bat had to get Ozzie shots.

Ozzie Osbourne.

The sixties' decade may be remembered for its fashion, music, freedom of speech, politics, the years that shaped a generation and more, but it was also the decade that television made some ground breaking advancements. It became a part of family life and brought the world into our living rooms. Sixties' television, together with the advancement of political journalism, became a political force, reaching a broader audience, with everything from talk and variety shows, to movies and debates addressing serious issues of the time.

Just as the world underwent dramatic social and cultural change during that decade, so television led the way in reflecting the Swinging Sixties. Television in the early 1960s was very different to now. We tend to forget that television at that time was black and white, and not only that, there was only one channel '*BBC*'! We forget, too, that TV was not broadcast twenty-four hours a day, as it is now. Today, it is often switched on continuously, even if nobody is watching it, or we are busy doing something else, but in the early sixties you would schedule time for it or turn it on for specific shows.

Over a very short period of time, working-class families in Britain began to have the choice of news, politics, sports and entertainment in way of shows, films, documentaries to suit the whole family. It was simple to begin with, you watched what the network put on and that was it. Later, around 1967, when ''commercial television' arrived, and shortly after ‘colour TV’, too, there were several new channels, and a considerable choice of programmes. This was fine, except it created ‘heated’ family discussions as to which programme each person wanted to watch. Even at that time, not every family had a television, so it was not unusual to receive unexpected visits from friends or neighbours that arrived just at the time a popular show or important sports event was coming on air.

The sixties were also the golden age of British humour, which, through television, reached out to audiences worldwide. It was at this time, many TV comedy shows, typical of British culture, became internationally popular and the television, an important channel for the export of British humour, to an international audience. There are few things the Brits will not joke about. We use humour to lighten even the most embarrassing, unfortunate, miserable moments, in fact, we turn to laughter as a form of medicine, which may not be the case with many other cultures, and the reason our humour has become popular worldwide.

With television beginning to lead the way in reflecting British culture and the absurdity of everyday life, audiences began to understand and appreciate that our humour is a reflection of the stability of our society, with a strong element of satire aimed at the various class systems, sexual taboos, politics and everyday life.

A radio programme for adults, which was airing during the fifties, was to change the face of British comedy for years to come and still maintains influence today. ‘*The Goons*’ burst onto the radio with odd outlandish stories, absurd puns, catchphrases, and ground-breaking sound effects. The stories were a take on authority, the stupidity of people from all walks of life and a ludicrous view of the world. ‘The Goons’ was initially formed by three loveable, stupid, extroverts, namely, Spike Milligan, Peter Sellers, and Harry Secombe, a fusion of Irish, English and Welsh cultural humour, who invented characters such as Major Bloodnok, Eccles, Minnie Bannister and Bluebottle.

Secombe and Milligan became friends whilst serving in the army during the Second World War. The story goes that their first meeting was when Milligan, who served as a gunner somehow allowed the large Howitzer gun he was attending to fall over the edge of a cliff, under which Secombe was sitting in a small radio truck. It goes that there was a terrible noise as some large object fell from the sky landing close to the truck. After some confusion, some idiot with a helmet on, Milligan peered in the truck, and asked, "Anyone seen a gun?" To which Secombe answered, "What colour was it?" This type of satirical humour later transferred to television shows, such as the, '*At Last the 1948 Show*', which had nothing to do with that year, and '*Monty Python's Flying Circus*', whose sketches were anything from absurd to obscure that milked the humour out of anything they came across, with sketches such as *The Dead Parrot*, *The Ministry of Funny Walks* and *the Spam*, or *Always Look on the Bright Side of Life* songs. This was the beginning of the Golden age of British comedy.

A television programme, which I found amusing, even though I was young at the time and it was above my level of intelligence, but very popular with adults, was a satirical news comedy, '*That Was the Week That Was*'. *TWTWTW* first went on air in November 1962, hosted by a very young David Frost (his first TV programme), and was an instant success due to its mockery of the establishment and political figures of that period. No other satire, news, discussion comedy series has ever come anywhere near to the enjoyment this programme brought, and neither could it now with today's political correctness. It would be difficult for people today, to understand what an impact TWTWTW had on the sixties' generation.

The programme did not lean towards any particular political party as news shows do today, but held nothing back in their sketches, songs and criticism to also ridicule world affairs, which covered anything from racism, Apartheid, the Ku Klux Klan to capital punishment. Nobody escaped, and targets lampooned included the Prime Minister, The Royal Family, the British Empire, the class system and its sexual and social hypocrisy. What else would you expect from a team of writers such as Bernard Levin, Peter Cook and John Cleese?

It's hard, now, to believe, that the BBC even aired such a satirical political programme, but they did. It ran for two seasons, before being pulled because of the upcoming 1964 general election, the reason given, was that the show's political material could compromise the BBC's impartiality.

Following TWTWTW, David Frost became a very famous television presenter and well known for his contribution to British culture. He worked as a host on US television, where he interviewed senior political figures, the most famous of these ex US President, Richard Nixon. The Nixon interviews were recorded and televised in 1977, where he asked Nixon blunt questions about the legality of his actions in the Watergate Scandal, and got him to explain and apologies for what he did. Sir David Frost OBE died of a heart attack whilst on a cruise, aboard the M.S. Queen Elizabeth II in Mediterranean Sea, during August 2013.

The Watergate Scandal occurred early 1972, during and after the Presidential Elections, when it was discovered that FBI and CIA agents had broken into the offices, tapped the phone lines and stole secret documents of Democratic candidate George McGovern, who was standing against Republican Richard Nixon.

Forty-five million people are said to have watched the Watergate interview, becoming at that time, the most-watched interview in the history of television.

Peter Cook and Dudley Moore contributed greatly to a new satire style of comedy during the sixties, with their stubborn ill-informed take on life. '*Not only...But Also*', was probably their most popular series, which aired for three seasons from 1965. Their scripts were not written in stone, and showcased 'Pete', with his boring nasal voice and know-it-all attitude, discussing with 'Dud', his dim-witted, scruffy friend, all kinds of topics he thought he knew all about, with Dud agreeing with him, commenting and asking all kinds of dumb, but sometimes-relevant questions (which Pete had to find an answer for). The sketches were, in most part, ad-libs, and sometimes the most amusing parts were their reactions, and them trying to hold back laughter when surprised by an unrehearsed jibe or comical remark by the other. Both Cook and Moore had separate careers, with Cook a writer and a founding member of the satirical current affairs magazine '*Private Eye*', founded in 1961, and Moore an accomplished pianist and musician, going on to appear in a number of films.

Situation comedies became very popular during the mid-sixties, and classics such as '*The Army Game*', '*Steptoe and Son*', and '*Dads Army*' (which enjoys repeats and still entertains audiences today), is a series which features awkward but humorous events of the Local Defence Volunteers, that became known as the Home Guard, which, due to the vast number of elderly volunteers, it also earned the nickname of 'Dad's Army'. As if the Germans and the constant threat of invasion aren't enough to deal with, the platoon have their own local and self-inflicted problems. The platoon are based in Walmington-on-Sea, a small town on the south coast of England, led by Captain George Mainwaring, the ostentatious local branch manager of Swallow Bank. The main body of the platoon is comprised of a number of regular privates. The most notable of these are a mummy's boy and bank clerk, a pessimistic Scottish undertaker, a black-market Cockney spiv, and an elderly medical orderly, who (all because of age or disability), cannot join the armed forces. Despite all that age, war, and their own pomposity, infighting and incompetence throws at them, these fine boys make up England's last line of defence against a Nazi attack. God help us if they did.

Another classic, which was hilarious and true of family life at the time, but cannot be repeated today, again, because of today's cultural issues, was '*Till Death Us Do Part*', which ran for seven series between 1965 and 1975, and was one of the most controversial comedies of its time and possibly remains so until this day.

The show focused on the day-to-day lives and opposing political and racial opinions of the Garnett family, led by, reactionary, white, working-class, Cockney Alf Garnett. Alf was an opinionated old man who held racist and anti-socialist views. Then, there was his gentle and long-suffering wife Else (who he referred to as the silly old moo). A conversation with Else from the show went like this…

Alf Garnett (tapping the newspaper with the headline '*The Million Pound Queen*'): Course, she needs the money. She's broke, Er Majesty.

Else Garnett: And I am!

Alf Garnett: I mean, look at Royal Ascot. She had to turn up in a horse and cart. Everybody else in their bleeding Rolls-Royces. Bloody Wilson. Darlin Arold. He's bankrupt her. (*Wilson being Prime minister at the time)*

Else Garnett: So you say.

Alf Garnett: So, I say? So, I say? Will you shut up, you stupid pie-can? Not a question of what I say. It's facts, innit?

And there was his dizzy daughter Rita and Rita's bright, but lazy, longhaired, lay-about husband Mike, (often referred to as a Scouse git). Mike was a socialist and loved to wind Alf up with his political and social views. In one episode discussing immigration, Alf says to Mike, "That's why they have foreign countries, for foreigners to live in, idiot!" The pair would constantly fall out over football, with Mike, a Liverpool supporter, making sarcastic remarks about Alf's beloved football team, West Ham. The character Alf Garnett became a well-known character in British Culture.

Mike, the Scouse git (actor Tony Booth), was the father of Cherie Blair and father-in-law to ex-prime minister Tony Blair. He was a political activist, and often spoke out against his son-in-law's government and against the Iraq War.

There were definite 'family favourites' on certain nights of the week. Two examples that come to mind are '*Sunday Night at the London Palladium*', which was compered over the years, by people like Tommy Trinder, Tommy Cooper, Norman Wisdom, Bruce Forsyth, and several more. But, apart from the '*Tiller Girls*' dancing act, there was always '*Special*

Guest Stars', such as The Beatles or Shirley Bassey, that were very much anticipated.

Another popular programme of the day was '*This Is Your Life*', compered for many years by Eamon Andrews. It was a marvellous programme because the 'guest star' was completely unaware of the fact that they were about to be 'starring' in a TV programme! They were somehow 'tricked' into the studio, where suddenly Eamon would appear and announce (for example) 'Albert Smith World War II Hero, holder of the Military Cross for gallantry during active operations against the enemy, father of five etc. etc.', 'This is Your Life'! Much to the shock-astonishment of the particular guest. Eamon would then go back through the 'guest's' life and introduce many of their relatives and friends from the past.

A show, some years later, went a little pear-shaped, when rockstar Garry Glitter, who achieved popular success in the 1970s, was the guest. Glitter eventually fell from grace for possessing child pornography and activities with an underage girl. He later faced criminal charges for child abuse in Cambodia and Vietnam. During the show, Glitter became exposed, during a chilling moment when the daughter of a friend appeared and innocently went on to tell the audience how, when Glitter, who was out of work, was staying at their home, she would bring her school friends around (dressed in their school uniforms) to meet him. A shocked and embarrassed Glitter can be seen putting his finger to his lips, urging her to be quiet.

A couple of adventure series worth a mention that aired during the sixties and were ahead of their time are '*The Avengers*' and '*The Prisoner*'.

The Avengers began as a conventional spy series and transformed into one of the most bizarre and inventive drama series ever made. The main character was a bowler-hatted secret agent, by the name of Steed, who would thwart the plans and save the world from diabolical schemes of evildoers. His karate kicking assistant Emma Peel, in her miniskirts and leather boots, is still considered one of the strongest female characters ever seen on British television.

The Prisoner was once described, "As one of those things that inspires either absolute devotion or utter confusion. There is no halfway!" The Prisoner (known only as number six) was a former government agent who resigned from his job and imprisoned in a beautiful and charming, yet secretive, enigmatic community in a mysterious isolated village. He is wanted for the top-secret information he knows. He is constantly trying to escape but each time is exposed by a mysterious glowing balloon type device that hovers overhead. My recollections of this series were that each time his number was called out over the tannoy system, he would respond, "I am a name I am not a number." However, I never remember if or how he eventually escaped. Two other series airing at this time, '*The Saint*' and '*Danger Man*' just go to show the quality of British Television all those years ago.

First aired during 1963, "Doctor Who" was another series considered ahead of its time, which went on to run for a number of years and has a cult following to this day, although it was not a series that I followed. It was a science fiction program whereby an extra-terrestrial being 'The Doctor' having the appearance of an eccentric human, travelled through time and the universe, (well that's how I understood it) in a space ship which had the appearance of a Blue British Police Box, which were common around towns at that time. The Doctor and his crew, would encounter alien species in unknown planets. The space ship would change its appearance depending on its surroundings.

The thing I remember most about the series were the Daleks. The Daleks portray themselves as the supreme race. They are villains that want to do away with non-Dalek existence and believe that no creature is superior to them. They are violent, ruthless, merciless aliens bent on exterminating any race that do not conform. (Similar to some earthling groups that exist today). The Daleks are the size of humans, encased in an armoured robotic body below a rotating cylindrical dome, which encases the eye. Protruding below are a gun-stick (type of ray-gun) and a telescopic plunger which has many uses such as measuring the intelligence of other beings and extracting information from the minds of their enemies.

The Daleks took the country by storm, not just the younger generation. Friends would greet you in the street by saying in a crackly Dalek voice, "You are an enemy of the Daleks, you are inferior you will be exterminated" others would shuffle up to you imitating a Dalek with an arm out pointing a finger (The ray-gun) saying, "I am a Dalek, exterminate, exterminate". Parents would tell their children to go for a bath or clean up their room and the response with an outstretched arm (The ray-gun again firing destructive energy) pointing at them and in a stuttering Dalek voice would be "Daleks have no concept of cleanliness and do not take orders from humans"!

The sixties was also the decade in which some major soap operas were created, such as '*The Newcomers*' and '*Crossroads*', with the most popular being '*Coronation Street*', which was a representation of daily life in a northern working-class community.

Coronation Street, which first aired on British TV December 1960, till this day, remains at the top of audience ratings and is probably the longest-running series in the world. It was, however, never a programme that I enjoyed. The theme music, in spite of being the most played theme tune on British TV, to me, was the most depressing. How anyone can listen to it several times a week without putting their foot through the screen, I will never know. I can almost relate to that person who wrote to the producers and said that *when they hear that music they want to cry and stab themselves in the face*. The music, together with the images of dull damp, terraced houses, to the depressing story lines and drab characters, rates in my top ten memories of 60s boring TV viewing. It definitely runs alongside my other memories of sitting at home on dark cold wet Saturday winter afternoons, when the only entertainment was horse-racing, where one would wait over half an hour between races, listening to the betting odds, watching the horses parade around the paddock, before slowly trotting towards the starting gate, and the race, when it finally started, lasted only two or three minutes.

The horseracing was followed by rugby league or wrestling. The rugby league commentator was Eddie Waring, who would somehow make the game of two teams of grumpy, irritable, stocky, chubby, overweight guys, with cauliflower ears and broken noses, fighting and gouging over an odd shaped ball in the cold rain and mud, in such places such as Wigan or Wakefield, a little more interesting. Many of his comments, in his Yorkshire accent, became catchphrases such as "*Goo on lad, git stuck in*", "*It's an up and under*" and "*He's taking an early bath*" i.e. been sent off (I am aware, of course, that these days, the game of rugby is much improved, with both the fitness and discipline of the players, as to the rules and improved conditions of the stadiums).

The wrestling was somewhat more entertaining, with the likes of Johnny Kwango, an ex-professional ballet dancer, with a travelling dance group, originally the first all-black dance group in Europe. Kwango was known as the King of head butts and for doing the splits in the ring, and there was Mick McManus, the wrestler that the fans '*loved to hate*', or 'Billy Two Rivers', a Canadian Mohawk Indian, who, when agitated, would perform an Indian war dance inside the ring in front of his opponent.

Today, when I remember those Saturday afternoons, all those years ago, I see a young lad sitting in front of the TV, bored and frustrated, who wanted to be outside, getting into mischief with his mates, playing or watching his beloved football team, Coventry City, or wandering around the city centre, looking for girls, instead of being stuck in the house on a drab winters afternoon because of lack of funds or the miserable British weather.

There was a weekly entertainment and variety show that was very popular during the sixties, which no doubt would be condemned today, a show which I would watch in total bemusement. The show aired for two decades, with an audience reaching 18 million viewers at its height. Until today, many still refer to the show as the least politically correct show ever put out by the BBC. A spokesman for The Commission for Racial Equality once said that the shows are anachronistic, and many people find them distasteful.

The '*Black and White Minstrel Show*' would run non-stop for 45 minutes on Saturday evenings. I think it's fair to say that it was pure, old-fashioned entertainment, and it did not set out to be racist. The idea was simply imported from America, were minstrels had been entertaining audiences for years. The show was performed by white singers that had blackened faces, with eyes and lips exaggerated with white paint. With black woolly wigs, white gloves, tailcoats, sometimes in ragged clothes, they would impersonate the travelling negro minstrel groups of the past, from America's deep south. They would perform such songs as, '*Dixie*', '*Swanee River*', '*Camptown Races*' and, '*Mammy*'. Guest performers did not blacken their faces, and the supporting female troupe remained pink and blonde, which was visually striking when colour TV was introduced later. Even so, there was controversy in some quarters, as some sketches they performed could be interpreted to be negro slaves wooing rich landowners' white daughters or wives.

On 18th May 1967, The Campaign Against Racial Discrimination presented a petition to the BBC, signed by both black and white people, demanding that the programme be taken off the television. Despite the controversy, the show's popularity continued, and it went on until 1978, where it was taken off air, which is thought to be as much for the demise of popular entertainment, low ratings and budgets, as the racial thing.

We should not forget that Al Jolson, who was considered as the first 'superstar' before the phrase was coined, blacked up, and performed just as the Black and White Minstrels did. He was loved by both black and white because he had such a wonderful voice. He also became known for fighting against black discrimination on the Broadway entertainment scene.

Whilst on the subject of blacked faces, I read that the annual Shrewsbury Folk Festival recently banned Morris Dancers from performing with blacked faces, after the festival organisers received a complaint from a member of the public complaining that this 500-year-old tradition is racialist! How sad is that?

Morris dancers have performed with blackface make-up since the origins of the dancing tradition, which is thought to date back to the 16th century. Known as 'Border Morris', the tradition sees performers wearing a full-face of black paint, in order to disguise themselves. But it has no racial connotations. One theory is that it started when impoverished 16th century farm workers had to conceal their faces to avoid being recognised while begging during winter months, as asking for money was illegal.

So, what about the wooden sticks (batons) the dances carry, should they then be banned as being offensive weapons?

Children's entertainment became varied and entertaining over the decade, with weekly children's variety shows, with music games and prizes, such as '*It's Friday It's Five to Five It's Crackerjack*'. What I remember most about the show is the quiz, where two or three kids would compete on the stage. Every time they got an answer right, they would receive a prize, a wrong answer, they would get a cabbage. The kids would accumulate armfuls of prizes piled high. Dropping the prizes or two wrong answers meant they were out.

'*Thunderbirds*' was an exciting secret international rescue organisation (a marionette puppetry science fiction production), dedicated to saving lives. The highly advanced Thunderbird craft would go on daring missions to save lives and rescue aircraft or spaceships that were in serious danger.

Who can talk about the sixties, in retro, without mentioning 'Billy Bunter', that likable fat schoolboy rogue of Greyfriars School, or the fearless pirate, 'Captain Pugwash', who sailed the high seas in his ship, 'The Black Pig'?

Bunter's character was of a devious, mischievous, greedy fat, short and round schoolboy, in old-fashioned school uniform, typical of that era, with a school cap and round spectacles. He was very anti-establishment in his own way. Bunter would keep us entertained by his pranks of skiving from attending cricket, falling asleep during lessons, stealing the other boys' cakes and sandwiches, and any food he came across, and writing rude things on the blackboard, but always in denial that it was him. The stories were once described as suitable for children from six to ninety-six! He regularly received six of the best (canings) from the Head Master, Mr Quelch. *Do I have to say, again, that this is another programme that most probably would not air today in its original form, because of today's social in-correctness?*

Captain Pugwash was the simplest of entertainment and produced in the most basic fashion – using cut out puppets, making the simplest of movements against static backgrounds. Levers were used to help the characters move their eyes, mouths and limbs, and the ship rock. The series had a memorial theme tune, '*The Trumpet Hornpipe*', and each episode aired for only five minutes in the evening, between children's and adult viewing time. The whole family would stop what they were doing and watch, with a mixture of amusement and awe on how Pugwash and the hapless crew of his ship, the 'Black Pig', would ward off his arch-enemy 'Cutthroat Jake'. Jake was a bearded pirate with an eye patch, and skipper of the pirate ship, '*Flying Dustman*'. Captain Pugwash, himself, was not a very good pirate, and his master, mate and crew were worse. In fact, Cutthroat Jake always seemed to have more treasure than them. Lucky for them, however, Tom the Cabin Boy, who looked after the crew, cooked the meals and sometimes navigated the ship, was the one with the brains who advised the Captain and got them out of sticky situations, but Pugwash always gave himself the credit. Pugwash was renowned for his exclamations, such as '*Dolloping dolphins*', '*Kipper me, capstans*', '*Blistering barnacles*', and so on. Cutthroat Jake who spoke with a strong

English West Country accent, would occasionally throw out expressions such as *Scupper me, Skull and Crossbones*.

As I wrote earlier, there are many reasons our sixties' generation grew up different! Where has our sense of humour gone?

Many TV shows at that time were broadcast live.

'*Blue Peter*' was a live children's magazine entertainment show that started in 1958 and went on to be the longest-running children's TV show in the world and was a significant part of British culture. The programme was aimed at kids, up until the age of fourteen years, with different topics on how to make things at home out of junk, music from glass bottles, how to care for pets, arts and crafts and presenters' challenges. I remember Blue Peter most for the episode when Lulu the young elephant appeared, and not only stole the show, but created a slice of television history.

The presenters at the time were John Noakes, Valerie Singleton and Peter Purves, all very relaxed and excited about having Lulu on the show. Lulu was a baby elephant of enormous strength, Lulu's keeper. 'Smithy', was a tiny chubby elderly gentleman, dressed in uniform. The TV presentation begins with the three presenters in front of the camera, and Valerie telling the viewers, "In today's programme we are going to show you some very interested things." At that, moment Lulu appears in the background with Smithy the keeper in tow, obviously having difficulty in containing her. The sequence of events went something like the following…

They introduce Lulu and all is under control, as Valerie gives her a bucket of water to drink, and explains that every day, Lulu is given twelve pints of milk and three buckets of water to drink.

John and Valerie stand at the rear of Lulu, while she drinks the water and Valarie continues talking about elephants.

Lulu then decides to urinate, flooding the studio floor and splashing the presenters standing behind her.

Peter mentions that they are having a slight problem and Valerie thanks Smithy, indicating that Lulu's time is up.

Smithy pulls Lulu around to lead her away, exposing her rear end, but before leaving, Lulu decides to take a baby elephant-sized 'dump' in front of the camera.

The three presenters, standing in the urine, facing the camera, are talking about a following topic, where in the background, Smithy can be seen, struggling with Lulu. She doesn't want to go anywhere.

Lulu turns around and pulls a struggling little Smithy back to the front of the studio floor, pushing Peter and Valerie out of her way.

Smithy, again, tries to lead Lulu off of the set, but again, she pulls him back to the front of the studio floor, pushes Peter out of the way and poses in front of the camera, in front of the three presenters.

The presenters have no choice but to accept that Lulu doesn't want to go anywhere and wants to be star of the show. They stand with Lulu and Valerie continues in her sweet voice, "The one thing that we must be sure of, is that our animals are going to be as happy as we are," when, Lulu becomes a little agitated, pushing Peter out of the way, followed by John shouting, "Aw, get off me foot."

Lulu then decides she wants to go on a walk about, with Smithy, who is desperately hanging on, until he slips on his arse in Lulu's mess and is dragged along the studio floor which, is now like an ice rink.

John and Peter help Smithy to his feet, where he tries to stand to attention, like all good men do in such circumstances, but Lulu trots off and disappears from the screen, with Smithy in tow.

John Noakes, relieved, shouts out, "And there she goes!" Just as he steps back and stands in a pile of elephant shit.

And then, there were those amazing travel, adventure and exploration documentary series, which, for the first time, brought the natural world in to our homes. Indigenous tribes, wild animals, birds of paradise and exotic places were no longer a myth or a picture in a book, they actually existed.

The world was a far bigger place and less travelled, all those years ago, and so much was waiting to be discovered. Enthralled, I would watch programmes such as '*Zoo Quest*', with David Attenborough (now '*Sir David*'). He would take us on adventures to discover places with wonderful names like Madagascar, Borneo, New Guinea or along the Zambezi River. He introduced us to the fascinating Indonesian Island of Bali, with its festivals, religious rituals, customs and exotic dances. We learned about the Pigmies of the Congo, Head Hunters and Giraffe Women. It was Attenborough that gave the world the first known footage of the 'Komodo Dragon'. The Komodo dragon is a lizard that can only be found on the Indonesian Komodo Islands. It can grow to a length of three meters, weigh 70 kg and hunts or ambushes birds and mammals.

My favourite story of his, is his encounter in Papua New Guinea with a tribe of cannibals. It was during an expedition deep into the jungle when his local native guides refused to go any further. Through the interpreter, it was explained that they were in head hunter's territory. As he was trying to convince them to continue, around sixty angry-looking natives suddenly jumped out on to the trail in front and ran down towards, them brandishing spears and knives. In his words, "*to say I was alarmed is to put it mildly*," he goes on to say, "*I walked towards this screaming horde of natives, and when they stopped in front of me, I held out my hand to them, and I heard myself say...good afternoon*!"

On Safari with Armand and Michaela, Denis gave us our first live images of life in Africa and revolutionised wildlife documentaries on television. They travelled together in a jeep and the early series were black and white and silent but narrated by themselves. I remember Armand for his strong accent and Michaela for her sexy voice.

Diving adventures with Jaques Cousteau from his ship, the Calypso, were absolutely fabulous. He created a series, '*The Undersea World of Jaques Cousteau*', where they go on voyages, exploring various underwater regions around the world to search, uncover and film unknown secrets of the deep. Cousteau went on to produce more than one hundred and twenty television documentaries, write more than sixty books and form an environmental protection foundation with thousands of members.

News coverage came of age in the sixties. Television had been behind print journalism until people became to rely on TV news for the day's headlines, as well as other information as to what was happening in other parts of the world. When something happened and it appeared on TV, it affected the whole country at the same time. As time went, on TV reached a broader audience, became a political force and tackled serious issues.

The news and coverage of John F Kennedy's assassination in November 1963, on our television sets, was an example on how breaking news could be delivered immediately to all corners. The Vietnam War was the first war whereby uncensored coverage was transmitted directly into the homes of families all over the world. It is often described as the first television war where battles were brought directly into the living room.

News items such as a South Vietnamese General parading a suspected North Vietnamese communist soldier in front of the camera and executing him on the spot, with a bullet in the head, brought home to viewers the impact that TV was having on their lives.

And a 1972 newsreel, showing a little naked Vietnamese girl running down a road, her body scorched by napalm, escaping an American attack on her village.

The coverage level would be unmatched until the terrorist attacks on the World Trade Centre in New York in 2001.

Chapter 13
When Our City Turned Sky Blue

If the Titanic had been painted sky blue, it would not have gone down.

Coventry City Supporter.

It all started in 1961, following Coventry City Football Club's embarrassing FA Cup defeat to 'none league' club, King's Lynn, when a former Fulham FC player by the name of Jimmy Hill was watching from the stands that day.

What made him decide he wanted to manage a shower of losers, the team were at that time, only god knows, but thankfully he did. Jimmy Hill immediately made great changes to the club and the team's image, which became known as '*The Sky-Blue Revolution*'. Hill went on to guide the club from the third division, until they gained promotion, in 1967, to the English 1st Division (which later became the English Premiership), for the first time in the club's history. Stubbornly, Coventry City remained in the topflight for the next 34 years.

When Hill arrived as manager in 1961, he transformed everything about the club He was a superb man, not only for the club, but for the City of Coventry, and a pioneer for football, as a whole. The first thing he did was to change the colour of the strip to sky blue from the all-white that the team previously played in (hence the nickname 'Sky Blues'). He wrote the *Sky-Blue Song*, sung to the tune of the *Eton Boat Song*, which is still sung by city fans at matches, even today, more than fifty years later. He also brought in some fabulous new players.

With Coventry City, Hill introduced the first fully fledged, glossy, colour matchday programme in English football. He organised pre-match entertainment for the fans that arrived at the ground early. Coventry had the first electronic scoreboard in 1964, and later, was the first club to have an all-seater stadium at their Highfield Road ground. They were also the first to show a live match, via CCTV, on four giant screens. In the city, they renamed a street to Sky Blue Way, there were sky blue taxis, sky blue coach services, a sky-blue pub, even a train was laid on for away games – the Sky Blue Express.

And so, there we were, week in, week out, watching the top English teams of the sixties at our home ground in Coventry – the Manchester United's, the Liverpool's, the Leeds United's, the Arsenals and the Tottenham Hotspurs, and some of the finest players of that decade – the likes of Jimmy Greaves, George Best, Bobby Moor, Gordon Banks and Bobby Charlton. We had so many laughs over the years, and probably experienced more downs than ups.

Only those fans that support the smaller clubs, their home teams, really appreciate the excitement of going home from a game, after beating the top teams or carving out wins, while fighting against relegation. There was always a bond at Coventry, between the fans and the players, and we felt part of the club, which is more than can be said for those who support the big clubs today, just because of who they are and what they win. It's called glory hunting! Football, like religion, depends somewhat in where and what community you were born and raised in.

True football lovers enjoy the unfashionable clubs, from places where they grew up, or those passed on by their fathers that get to the topflight and challenge the best, only to be relegated after one or two seasons. With Coventry, it was different, we were fashionable, and we refused to go down. During the 1969-70 season, the bookmakers made us favourites to be relegated, but instead we qualified for Europe. Our clubhouse, however, did not gain trophies, and at the end of each season, we were normally battling against relegation.

Supporting a football team is not just about winning every game. You have to support your team through the highs and lows. If you haven't sat on a cold wet windy night and watched your team lose, then how is it possible to feel true excitement when they win. But football is more than that, it's about, beer, pie and chips, comrade, travelling all over through thick and thin, to curious towns such as Yeovil, Scunthorpe and Rochdale, places you would otherwise have no reason to visit. It's about being proud of one's roots. There is no better feeling than supporting your home team, rather than a team you have no connection with.

How I miss those match days, in all kinds of weather, waiting excitedly to take the bus into the city centre. There was an air of excitement around the city and in the working men's club or the Jaguar Pub, where I would meet my mates for some pre-match beers. We would update on the team sheets for that particular day, dispute the quality of players and talk tactics, we were all pundits and the more beers we drunk, the more excited we got, and the more we thought we understood about football. For good luck, we would always walk the exact same route to the ground, White Street, then into Hales Street, past Swanswell Park, via Hillfields, and through an alley next to some open ground, where a bunch of football hooligans would lay in wait on 'Pork Chop Hill', to confront any opposing fans that might venture into their territory, then into the ground's West End Stand behind the goal. It didn't matter too much who the opposition were on the day or who was playing, as we went to support our team. We would never believe that they might lose. But they did, quite often.

It was sometime early to mid-sixties that the UK gained its reputation for 'football hooliganism' – violence between rival fans, that some described as a social epidemic of violence. During the 1964 football, season there began a well-planned and organised pastime at games between rival supporters, called 'taking ends'. The grounds were not all seated at that time, and neither were the terraces separated. Each team had a core of rowdy, often-violent supporters, later to be known as '*firms*', that would stake out a goal end terrace at their club's ground as 'their own territory'. Coventry's firm were known as The Legion, and later The West End Boot Boys, Chelsea, Head Hunters or Shed Boys, Derby, Lunatic Fringe, Manchester United, Red Army, and so on. Millwall Bushwhackers were notorious, and by far the most violent, and maintained that status over the years. The Chelsea Shed boys were probably the best organised and somewhat sophisticated. They would enter grounds with a military style plan of attack in place. Many of the group would enter the ground well dressed, giving the appearance of smart young men, such as office clerks, to avoid suspicion from the wardens or the police, but with the intentions of causing havoc.

Taking ends was probably more common during local derbies that took place closer to home because of the amount of away supporters that would turn up. Coventry's local derbies would be with teams, and arch-rivals, such as Aston Villa, Wolverhampton Wanderers or Leicester City. Alliances were formed amongst the group of supporters that occupied the terrace behind the goal as they defended their territory. For many of these groups, taunting, intimidating the opposing supporters and defending their reputations became more important than the games they went to watch. Visiting supporters would be welcomed with chants, with intelligent, inventive lyrics such as, "*You're all a load of wankers*," or, "*You're gonna get your fucking heads kicked in*." Regularly, all hell would break loose during a match, when fans on one side of the stadium would rush the opposing fans side and try to take control of their section. But let's be honest, who didn't feel a sense of pride after watching the confusion, followed by a sea of sky-blue scarves being lifted above the crowd, and hearing the Sky-Blue Song being sung from the Villa's Holte End or the Wolves North Bank. Especially, as we had been in the shadows of those scum for so many years. It was a tit for tat exercise, they would come to our place and cause bedlam, and our firm would go to theirs and try to outdo whatever they had achieved at ours, and, as a result, fights regularly took place inside the stadiums.

Going to watch your team play at away games was often a case of safety in numbers. When arriving in another city by train or coach, it would not be unusual for gangs of opposing supporters to lay in wait, somewhere en-route to the stadium, where they would taunt, insult and throw missiles at the visitors. The local police forces would normally provide an escort to the ground to avoid any trouble between the two sides of supporters. It was not a good idea to stray away from the group, as one could get picked off like lions pick off wildebeest straying from the herd. In the meantime, members of the 'Firm' would be causing destruction somewhere in the town.

Football hooliganism escalated into the seventies, and dozens of innocent supporters were getting injured, which led to crowd segregation and fencing at football grounds in England. Manchester United supporters are not angels when their team is not winning, in fact, the Red Army caused mayhem at grounds, up and down the country, during the 1973-74 season, when they got relegated to the second division. Prime Minister Margaret Thatcher's response at that time was to set up a '*war cabinet*' to combat football hooliganism. As usual, the national media had a field day and were somewhat responsible for intensifying the problem nationwide, with headlines such as '*War Crazy Yobs Besiege Town*' or '*Sick Fans who only come to Terrorise*'. Which basically gave that sector of hooligans the prominence they were looking for.

A friend of mine once asked me if I could explain why football was so serious. He said, he had a neighbour who appeared to be the perfect husband and father, attended his garden, went to church on Sundays, worked in a bank and was an active member of the community. Well, he happened to attend a football match one time, and saw his neighbour close to him in the crowd. He explained how his neighbour had transformed into a beer swilling, vulgar monster, waving his fists in the air, and shouting things like, "*Get up you fucking fairy, he didn't touch you,*" or, "*The ref must be a fucking Welshman, he knows fuck all about football.*" I told him that while I couldn't explain what football does to people, I knew exactly and understood how his neighbour felt.

Travelling to watch your team winning at away games is very special. A game that I will never forget was when a few of us slipped out of the factory early one afternoon to go and watch Coventry play Derby County at their Baseball Ground stadium. It was the 1970 season, and Coventry were having a good run of results at the time, and we were excited to watch our new signing. Wilf Smith, who was bought from Sheffield Wednesday, who, at £100,000, was the most expensive fullback in Britain at the time.

It was an evening game, we arrived at Derby in good time and parked the car near the stadium, in time for a few pints of beer at a pub close to the ground. Later, as we were walking from the pub to the ground, there was a torrential downpour of rain, it was a freezing cold night and we got drenched through. It was still raining when the game started, and within a few minutes and his first touch of the ball, our £100,000 full back Smyth got clogged, and was stretchered out. During the time we were down to ten men, Derby scored, and ten minutes later, scored another. At 2 x 0 down, surely that was it! We stood on the terrace, dejected, freezing cold and wet, arguing amongst ourselves as to whose stupid idea it was to come and watch this shower of idiots. However, after around half an hour, the City scored, and then, just before half time another. We were still in it! The second half started, and within ten minutes, City went ahead for the first time with a header from our centre forward. Our celebrations were short lived, when Derby County equalised shortly after that with a lucky shot, when the ball flew into the goal off of the back of a City player. All square!

Just when it looked like we were going to snatch a draw, a City defender elbowed a Derby player off the ball, inside the penalty area. Penalty to Derby. Derby's Penalty taker, 'Alan Hinton', who boasted one of the most explosive shots in football, stepped up. We were stood right behind the goal; it was a stomach-churning moment. Hinton put the ball to our goalkeeper's right, but the City's keeper, 'Bill Glazier', dove full length, and turned the ball outside.

City were hanging on for a draw. Derby had two goals disallowed for offside, a shot that hit the bar and one headed off the line. With two minutes to go, and us relieved to go away with a draw, City's redheaded Scotsman, 'Willie Carr', blasted the winner to give us victory.

And there we are, driving gloriously away from the ground, each of us denying that we ever doubted that Coventry could win, when a very large figure appeared out of the darkness in front of the car, signalling for us to stop. The car door opened, and the biggest cop's head I ever saw peered in. He looked at all six or seven of us, sitting on top of each other (it was a small Hillman Imp), and said to the driver, "What the fuck are you doing, driving the wrong way down a one-way street with no lights?" Chick, the driver, was speechless for a minute, and nervously replied, "I'm sorry, but we don't come from around here, we only came to see the game." The copper thought for a minute, and with a smirk on his face, replied, "I see, and where you come from don't, they have lights on cars or one-way streets?" We were all waiting for Chick's next words of wisdom when the cop said, "It smells like a brewery in here, now fuck off home to wherever you come from before I breathalyse and book you." I am sure that if we had been doing anything other than watching a football game the cop's decision would have been very different.

Coventry City finally did win a major trophy when they beat heavy favourites Tottenham Hotspur, a team full of international players in the 1987 FA Cup Final at Wembley Stadium. Interesting to note, that in contrast to many top teams of that time, the whole Coventry City squad, including the managers, were all English and one Welsh player.

After thirty-four years in the top flight, and a run of poor results, Coventry City were finally relegated from the English Premiership in 2001. There was a saying around the city for years that, *"If the Titanic had been painted Sky Blue, it wouldn't have gone down*." Sadly, Coventry City Football Club, today, are sinking lower into the depths of the English football divisions and are a shadow of the former. *It's good news, that during the time of writing and publishing this manuscript, Coventry City FC have move up a division and are well positioned to go further.*

Jimmy Hill OBE, football manager, football analyst, and one of the chief architects of the modern game in Britain, also credited with the introduction of the three points to win system, and using the first panel of football pundits for the 1970 World Cup, died of Alzheimer's disease December 2015, at the age of eighty-seven. A statue of Hill is located at Coventry's Ricoh Arena ground.

Today, the English Premier Football league is very popular, and games are transmitted live to countries, all over the world, and so I enjoy watching the games on the big screen, with friends in my local bar in Thailand. Thais are very passionate about their football, but normally support the most successful and well-known clubs. Sitting with them, however, I sometimes have to explain some of the finer aspects of the game.

Recently, we were in a bar, watching a big match between two of the top teams, and it was obvious that the young lady next to me was supporting Liverpool. At one point, Liverpool won a corner kick. Their player placed the ball next to the corner flag, stepped back a few paces, ready to take the kick. In the background, the camera caught a bunch of opposing fans, hanging over the barrier, shouting abuse at the player. Their arms were outstretched, with cupped hands, which they were vibrating. I, of course, knowing what they were suggesting, started laughing. The girl looked at me, and said, "What them guys doing? What they shouting?" I told her they were just supporters of the other team, trying to humiliate him. She was not satisfied with this and wanted to know every detail.

"Why they doing this with their hands?"

"They are just imitating something."

"What are they shouting at him?"

"Just something to make him feel inferior."

"So why they do this with their hands?"

"It's a sign telling him what they think of him."

"So, what do they think of him?"

There was no way she was going to let me get away with it, so I had to explain to her that they were shouting 'wanker', and they were imitating masturbation with their hands. Just a way of expressing their dislike of him and trying to belittle him.

Satisfied with my explanation, we continued to watch the game.

Sometime later, the game was in full flow, when one of the opposing players went into a crunching tackle, taking down a Liverpool player. My friend stood up, pointed to the big screen and in front of whole bar and like a true supporter, shouted, "Wankeerr!" The game continued for some time, when the referee blew his whistle, called a Liverpool player over to him and showed him a yellow card. She looked at me, and said, "What you call that man in the black shirt who do that?" I said he is the referee. She thought for a moment, looked at me, and with a serious expression, and said, "He is a wanker."

I am always happy to pass on a little British football culture on my travels.

Chapter 14
Events and Coming of Age

The struggles we endure today will be the 'good old days' we laugh about tomorrow.

Aaron Lauritson.

Someone once said that the 1960s was a decade of rapid change – blink for one second and you would miss something. I suppose, for me, it all started somewhere between 1963 and 1965, between leaving school and starting work. I started to become aware of what was going on around me, I listened to the radio, watched the news on TV and read the newspaper headlines. I would rise whilst it was still dark, around 05.30 a.m. make a mug of tea and listen to the radio, before doing my paper round and going to school.

There was the Profumo affair in 1963, when British Minister of War, 'John Profumo', denied having an affair with a prostitute, who at the same time, was sleeping with a Russian spy. It was cloak and dagger stuff, which engulfed the British government during the height of the Cold War (a time of political hostility between the Soviet Union, the US and the West).

Profumo later appeared before Parliament to say, "*With deep remorse*," that he had misled the House, and would resign from his post.

I must be honest, I was thirteen or fourteen years of age at the time, it was not the political events that got my attention, it was text that appeared in the newspaper articles such as sex scandal, prostitute, naked and sexual intercourse which drew my interest to the events. There were photographs of two good-looking prostitutes that were involved, Kristine Keeler and Mandi Rice-Davies, which excited me – seeing what real prostitutes looked like. There were stories of sex and frolicking naked in a swimming pool and dinner parties. There was an unknown man who served tables naked, except for a mask at dinner parties, put on by a man named 'Ward'. The man in the mask was rumoured to be a cabinet minister, but his name was never disclosed, and Ward, after being prosecuted for living on immoral earnings, killed himself with an overdose of pills. Kristine Keeler was also tried and imprisoned on related charges. I had to check the dictionary to understand the meaning of immoral earnings. How much I learned from reading these stories and how much they spiced up those drab mornings delivering newspapers! Until this day, however, I can't imagine who would want a naked man with a mask serving their dinner table. Unless, of course, they don't mind having his wedding tackle dangling in front of their face as he leans over to pour the wine.

One morning, early, sitting in the dark and supping my tea, the news came over the radio of a Royal Mail train that had been robbed on its way from Glasgow to London in the early hours. It became known as '*The Great Train Robbery*', one of the most infamous British robberies of all time. It was a brilliantly planned and executed robbery, with little violence except for an attack on the train driver who tried to resist. There were no firearms used. The gang got away with £2.6 million (in used bank notes), equivalent to around £49 million today, most of which was never recovered.

The robbery took place around 03.00 am on 8th August 1963, in Buckinghamshire, England, at a place called Sears Crossing. The railway line's green 'go' light was covered over, and a 6 volt Ever Ready battery connected to power the red 'stop' light, forcing the train to come to a halt. The gang, disguised in masks and dressed in boiler suits, boarded the train. They quickly uncoupled the first two carriages (where the money was stowed) from the rest of the train. There was a hick-up, when the gang member, who was to take control of the train realised, that the engine was a diesel and he was only familiar with steam, and so the driver was forced to shift the two carriages further along the line to where the money was unloaded. A number of royal mail sorting staff, that were occupying the rear carriages of the train, had no idea what was going on. The gang, making a human chain, loaded the more than one hundred sacks of money, more than one ton in weight, into two Land Rover vehicles and fled to a pre-arranged hide out, 'Leatherslade Farm', around 25 miles away. It was not until 04.15 that the alarm was raised as the railways phone line to the signalman along the line, had been cut.

The gang consisted of seventeen members who planned the robbery from inside information, provided by an unknown individual, only known as the Ulsterman, at the time. After the robbery, the men laid low at the farm, where, later, police were to find incriminating evidence that led to the arrest of most of the gang. The plan was to stay at the farm for a period of time, but they heard over the radio that the police were going to search every property within a thirty-mile radius of the crime scene, so they fled with their bags of cash, just before the police received a tip off from a nearby neighbour, about strange goings-on at the farm.

Some of the gang members were charged, based on evidence found around the farmhouse such as fingerprints found on a game of Monopoly (which they played with real money), playing cards and a pubic hair found in a sleeping bag used by one of the gang, others were let down by people they trusted, who informed the police, in spite of helping them hide their spoils. Everything was planned perfectly, and the gang would almost certainly have got away with it, except that many of the gang had not thought of or made plans on how or where to stash their money. Where do you stash around £2 million of cash? But it's ironic that their bad luck was that someone known as 'the Dustman', who had been paid a substantial amount to clear the evidence and set fire to the farm before the police arrived, didn't do it!

And, so, I followed the stories, day-by-day, during my paper round, as the various gang members were discovered one by one by the police, and arrested. Each arrest and gang member were a story of its own. I was intrigued on how the police tracked each of them down. One of the gang rented a garage and paid the rent three months in advance, all in ten-shilling notes, the owner became suspicious and tipped off the police, another stashed cash in bags and hid them in the woods, only to be found by a courting couple. The police found a receipt in one of the bags, with a name on it that lead them back to the gang member. The case went on into the following year, until most of the gang members were identified, tried and sentenced.

It was a unique and daring robbery that captured the imagination of the public for decades, not only in Britain, but all over the world. The general public were aggrieved at the excessive length of prison sentences given out to the ringleaders when they were tried and sentenced to thirty years in prison, which was much longer than those given to many murderers or armed robbers at the time. In those days, there was no parole or early release programme. Up to six of the alleged gang members escaped punishment, one way or another, and three were never caught.

There were many twists and turns, and until today, there are many unanswered questions surrounding the robbery

The mastermind Bruce Reynolds escaped to Mexico, but was arrested five years later, after secretly returning to Britain, whilst two of the gang escaped from the prisons where they were being held.

Ronnie Biggs was to become the most notorious of the robbers, when he escaped from Wandsworth Prison, some fifteen months into his sentence. One day, in July 1965, as a furniture van pulled up and parked alongside the walls of the prison, a door opened from the top and a rope ladder was thrown over the thirty-foot high wall, at the time the prisoners were taking their exercise, allowing four prisoners to scale the wall and escape, including Biggs. And so, another saga to entertain the British public begins. Biggs's escapades became a subject of numerous books, articles and films.

Biggs laid low in safe houses for five months, before escaping to Paris, where he underwent cheap plastic surgery, which troubled him for most of his life. Under a new name, he went to Australia and lived there for almost five years, until it was suspected that he was living there, and his photograph was shown on the national news. The same day, Biggs fled to a friend's house in the mountains, only hours before the police raided his home. Five months later, he boarded a ship to Panama, and via Caracas, travelled to Rio de Janeiro, Brazil.

Biggs settled comfortably into the Rio de Janeiro lifestyle, and became a celebrity, having no difficulty making friends. He became a tourist attraction, where people would pay for having their photograph taken with him, take him to dinner or buy mugs or t-shirts with his image or with an emblem, such as '*Rio, a Great Place to Escape'*. In the meantime, he got married to a Brazilian lady and they had a son.

Sometime later, Scotland Yard caught up with Biggs in Rio, and attempted to arrest him and bring him back to London. Detective Chief Superintendent 'Jack Slipper', who had been on Biggs tail from the beginning, offered him a deal and a fair trial on his return. Slipper, however, made the mistake of trying to arrest and extradite Biggs without the knowledge and authority of the Rio crimes department, otherwise undermining their authority. The authorities were not happy and, therefore, publicly announced that given Biggs was the father of a Brazilian child, they would not agree to Biggs extradition, and so Slipper returned to London emptyhanded.

That was not the last, as there was another attempt to get Biggs out of Brazil when a group of ex-British soldiers befriended him, before kidnapping him from a restaurant. He was trussed up in a sack and flown to the north of Brazil in a small plane, and by boat to Barbados. The kidnapper's boat broke down just off the coast of Barbados, where they were rescued by the local coastguard. Again, Biggs eluded arrest and extradition due to legal loopholes and returned to Brazil, kissing the tarmac on landing, to a typical Brazilian hero's welcome.

With his health deteriorating, and aware that he would be detained on arrival, Biggs, of his own accord, returned to

Britain on 7 May 2001, and was immediately arrested and detained. On 6th August 2009, he was released on compassionate grounds, and passed away on 18th December 2013, aged 84 at a care home in London, where he was being cared for.

He was cremated on 3rd January 2014. His coffin was draped with the Union Jack, a flag of Brazil and a scarf of his beloved football team, Charlton Athletic – his ashes are spread between England, Australia and Brazil.

The news headlines all over Britain, and English language papers all over the world, on 7th May 1966, read, 'Moors Murderers Ian Brady, and his lover, Myra Hindley, jailed for life'. Brady was twenty-seven, and his twenty-three-year-old girlfriend were suspected of abducting and killing five children. The murders were carried out between July 1963 and October 1965, in the Manchester area, England, but the bodies of only three were found by the time they were arrested in 1965. As the arrests were made shortly after Parliament abolished the death sentence in Britain, life sentences were the most they could receive.

The killings were known as '*The Moors Murders*', because the couple buried their victims in desolated areas on Saddleworth Moor, in the North of England. The grotesque details of sexual abuse, torture and beatings became apparent when police found a bag belonging to Brady in the left luggage at a Manchester train station. The contents were produced during the court hearings. Shocking evidence came to light, with pornographic photographs, and in one instance, a tape recording of a young victim pleading for her life. Sadly, the mother of the girl had to listen to the recording to confirm that it was in fact the voice of her young daughter. The public were horrified, and to this day, Brady and Hindley are remembered as the most hated couple in Britain ever. Their victims were aged between ten and seventeen, at least four of them had been sexually assaulted. One of the victims' graves was only discovered in 1987, more than twenty years after the trial. The body of another victim, that was never found, is suspected to be buried on the moor and Brady, up until his death, would never disclose the whereabouts. During their trial, the couple showed no empathy or remorse towards their victims and the families.

Brady and Hindley were arrested after the brother-in-law of Hindley saw Brady kill the seventeen-year-old boy (*I have refrained from giving the names of the victims),* and helped the couple to clean and remove the body. He later returned home and told his wife, Hindley's sister, about the incident, and the two reported it to the police.

The proposed minimum sentences, thirty years for Hindley and forty years for Brady, were criticised by Prime Minister Margaret Thatcher in 1985 when she said, "*Neither of them should ever be released from prison. Their crimes were the most hideous and cruel in modern times*."

They were never released. Hindley died 15th November 2002, at the age of sixty. (As many as twenty different undertakers refused to handle the body). She applied for parole on a number of occasions, which were denied. Hindley fell in love with and had an affair with one of her gay prison warders, who made a plan to help her escape. The plan was intercepted when copies of prison keys were found, and the warder was sentenced to six years in prison. Brady died 15th May 2017, aged seventy-nine. His ashes were disposed of at sea.

During June 1963, a young American heavyweight boxer by the name of Cassius Clay came to Britain to fight our British and European heavy weight champion at the time 'Henry Cooper'. We really did not know what to make of this mouthy young back guy, with the smooth Kentucky accent, who at the weigh-in appeared wearing a purple and gold crown declaring, "*You got a Queen in England, you need a King. I am the King!*"

The fight took place at Wembley Stadium on 18th June, and it was his first professional fight outside of the USA. Clay certainly got the attention of the British public, and it was the beginning of a lifelong love affair between him and this country. We had no idea then, that this guy would go on to become the greatest sportsman of all time, a person that understood that there are more important things than sport, which he went on to dedicate his life to, he was a fighter both inside the ring and he fought for what was right outside the ring. There is no celebrity, sports or movie star that brought so much happiness and excitement to those around him and to the places he visited, where he brought hope to so many.

Cassius Clay had no illusions at that time about declaring himself as '*The Greatest*', and that he was ready to become World Champion. He would wind-up the British public with his jibes about English life and his predictions for the fight. Whilst he may have irritated some, his humour and confidence stirred curiosity in others.

"It isn't no jive, Henry Cooper will go in five!" he predicted.

"Henry Cooper is nothing to me! If this bum goes over five rounds, I won't return to the United States for thirty days, and that's final!

"I'm not even worried about this big bum. Cooper will only be a warmup until I get to that big ugly bear, Sonny Liston!" (Liston was world heavyweight boxing champion at that time).

The fight turned out to be so remarkable that people still talk about it today. However, Ali got off on the wrong foot by upsetting us and our home favourite, when his trainer performed some ringside roguery between rounds.

The fight got off to a good start, with Cooper appearing to win the first two rounds, however, that's not to say Clay could have been pacing himself with his fifth-round prediction in mind. The third round was more even, although Clay drew first blood, with a firm right hand to Cooper's face, whilst Cooper was priming to deliver his famous left hook, known as '*Enery's Ammer*'. The fourth round continued just as the third, so we were left wondering what Clay had in store to finish the fight in the fifth, when, suddenly, it happened! A couple of seconds before the bell signalling the end of the fourth, Cooper connected with a vicious left hook that put Clay down, and halfway through the ropes, Clay slowly got to his feet, but had no idea where he was, and it looked unlikely he would recover in time to start the fifth round.

And here is where the confusion starts. Legend has it that Clay's trainer split the seam in one of Clay's gloves, and then brought it to the attention of the referee, asking for a change of gloves – he also used smelling salts to help Clay recover, which were deemed illegal at the time. The glove was not changed, as rumoured today, but the delay did buy enough time for Clay to recover and continue. Towards the end of the fifth round, however, Clay's prediction came true, when the referee stopped the fight, due to a nasty gash and blood gushing from over Coopers left eye.

After the fight, Clay's excuse for getting knocked down was, "*I was looking at Liz Taylor*," (a famous beautiful actress, at the time, who was watching from ringside) although, some years later, on British television, he said, "*Cooper hit me so hard that my ancestors in Africa felt it*."

Cassius Clay, on February 25th, 1964, at the age of 22 was crowned world boxing heavyweight champion at Miami Beach, Florida, after beating Sonny Liston in one of the biggest upsets in boxing history. Clay was the underdog, and it was unanimously believed that Clay would not survive two rounds, but Liston lost the fight, after refusing to come out for the seventh round.

Clay had, for some time, been a member of the (NOI) Nation of Islam, and after converting, changed his name to '*Muhammad Ali*', claiming Cassius Clay was his slave name, and so, when he returned to London in 1966 for a world heavyweight title fight with Henry Cooper, he arrived as Muhammad Ali.

Ali was up to his tricks again. When interviewed on a TV show being aired in Britain, he said, quote, "*Tell Henry Cooper, if he's watching this show, to come to the fight and be ready to fight because I'm coming to get you. I'm coming to London to get you. And after I'm through beating him, I think he'll have to join The Beatles and be a singer. I'm coming to get you, Henry. I don't like the way you knocked me down the last time. No man knocks me down and gets away with it, so you be ready for it, you hear? Be ready, because I'm coming to get you. Now, you go home, and tell him that. I'm not joking.*"

Their second fight took place at London's Highbury Stadium, 21st May 1966, and Ali retained his heavyweight title when the referee was forced to stop the fight during the sixth round, again due to another injury to Cooper's left eye.

After that, we would always wake up early or during the night and turn our radios or TV's on to listen to or hear that Ali had won his fights, in some faraway land.

During 1967, Muhammed Ali was stripped of his world heavyweight title for refusing to be inducted into the US Army and fight in Vietnam, claiming, "*I ain't got no quarrel with them Viet Cong, no Viet Cong ever called me a nigger,*" and cited that the war was against his religious and conscious beliefs. He returned to the ring in 1971 and went on to become a three-time world heavyweight champion.

Ali became a constant fixture in British lives, his sardonic sense of humour was not unlike our own. He fought more fights outside America in Britain than in any other country. Wherever he went, he would visit hospitals, schools, boxing clubs, and mosques to help them raise money; he was a constant guest on TV talk shows. My mother loved him and his humour, and would sit in front of the television, laughing at his quips, and telling my dad what a handsome man he was, whereas my dad would mumble under his breath how bloody stupid Ali was, when we knew he was too proud to admit to liking him.

Ali made an unforgettable visit to my hometown of Coventry during August 1983, where he was besieged by thousands of admirers wherever he went. Even he himself admitted being surprised at the crowds. After spending time opening shops, visiting clubs, etc. His visit concluded by visiting a simple fish and chip shop in a council estate, owned by an ex-sparring partner, 'Jack Bodell', whom he hadn't seen since 1966.

On 27th July 2012, possibly Ali's last public appearance in Britain, he was the titular bearer of the Olympic Flag at the

Summer Olympics in London. He had to be assisted by his wife, due to the Parkinson's disease that he had been fighting, since being diagnosed in 1984, rendering him unable to carry the flag alone. Sadly, Ali lost his last fight to Parkinson's disease and passed away at the age of seventy-four on 3rd June 2016.

Ali will also be remembered for his quotes, the most well-known is probably, "I float like a butterfly and sting like a bee, you can't hit what your eyes can't see," but a few others have given me inspiration over the years such as…

"*The fight is not won inside the ring, it's won or lost outside the ring, those many hours training in the gym, and out there on the road, long before I dance under the lights.*"

"*I only start counting the sit ups, when it starts to hurt.*"

"*It isn't the mountains ahead to climb that wear you out, it's the pebble in your shoe.*"

"*Friendship is not something you learn in school, But, if you haven't learned the meaning of friendship, you really haven't learned anything.*"

"*The man who views the world the same at fifty as he did when he was twenty has wasted thirty years of his life.*"

The biggest news headline of the sixties' decade, and possibly the most infamous event in US political history, prior to the 9/11 New York Trade Tower attacks, was the assassination of President John F Kennedy, which took place in Dallas, during 22 November 1963. I remember I was in my bedroom, listening to my Rolling Stones discs, when my brother burst in shouting, "They shot President Kennedy!" And I don't know why, he said, "There's going to be a war!" I didn't pay much attention to it, at the time, but I do remember seeing the news coverage, which later was acknowledged as the moment television news came of age.

Kennedy's motorcade was moving slowly along a street lined with waving crowds and Kennedy was waving to them, with his arm raised over the side of the car, when shots rang out and bullets entered his head and neck. He fell forward into the arms of his wife Jacqueline. The car sped off to a hospital, which was just a few minutes away, where President John F Kennedy was, a short time later, pronounced dead.

It's ironic, that just a moment earlier, the first lady of Texas, who was sitting in front of him, turned to him, and said, "*Mr President, you can't say Dallas doesn't love you,*" to which the President responded by saying, "*No, you certainly can't.*" Those were the last words ever spoken by John Kennedy.

An ex-marine and self-proclaimed Marxist by the name of Lee Harvey Oswald was later arrested and charged with the murder of Kennedy, to which he denied, claiming he was being made a scapegoat, however he never stood trial. Two days later, on the morning of 24th November, whilst in the process of being transferred from the city jail to the county jail, Oswald was fatally shot. Millions of viewers across America that were watching live coverage were stunned to see this bizarre aftermath, when Jack Ruby, a local night club owner, stepped out of a crowd of onlookers, aimed a pistol and fired at point-blank range. Oswald died two hours later.

Ruby claimed that he acted impulsively and shot Oswald out of grief, however, many believe he killed him to prevent him from revealing multiple members of a larger conspiracy to assassinate Kennedy. Jack Ruby was found guilty of the murder of Oswald and was sentenced to death by electric chair. Ruby appealed the sentence on the fact he could not have received a fair trial in Dallas at the time but died of lung cancer in 1967, whilst awaiting a new trial to be arranged.

Until this day, the question remains; why did Oswald kill Kennedy, and what were his motives? How did this skinny kid pull it off and fire three accurate shots in eight seconds, using a bolt-action rifle? How could the second shot hit Kennedy in the back, exit his neck, then strike a second person in the back, and come out of their chest? The majority of Americans, over 60%, do not believe Lee Harvey Oswald assassinated Kennedy, although the FBI would like them to think he did.

President Kennedy was considered to be a youthful, glamorous leader. He promised to do all he could to bring hope, peace and freedom to every American, an end of tyranny, and war, and to lead America into a better future, although, the myth was built around him, more so after his death. The records, however, show that during his term, he passed no domestic legislations of any significance, did little for civil rights. Some thought him responsible for causing the Cuban Missile Crisis and doing nothing to defer the Vietnam War.

He endorsed a coup in 1963 for the South Vietnamese military to overthrow the then-South Vietnamese President, Ngo Dinh Diem, in order to have more American involvement in that country. Kennedy did this without first conferring with his chief political advisers. Diem, who was promised a safe passage out of the country, was immediately assassinated by the military, which made an already bad situation in the south worse. Once, when questioned about the merits of staying in Vietnam his answer was, "*I can't be expected to give up a piece of territory like Vietnam and get people to re-elect me!*" The things that I do remember were that Kennedy promised to put a man on the Moon before the end of the decade, which at that time could only be termed as, 'wishful thinking', and, that he coined the phrase, "*You don't ask what your country can do for you, you ask what you can do for your country!*"

Jacqueline Kennedy, to this day, remains one of Americas most popular First Ladies. During her husband's presidency, she became known as a trendsetter for her choices of fashion and love of arts, she also became known for her highly publicised restoration of the White House. Her style fit well into the sixties' culture of that period.

Five years after John Kennedy's assassination, the world was astonished with the news that Jacqueline was to marry a long-time friend, Aristotle Onassis, twenty-three years her senior. Onassis was a Greek shipping magnet, who owned the world's largest privately-owned shipping fleet and was one of the world's richest and most famous men. The wedding took place on the Island of Skorpios. Onassis passed away in Paris, during March 1975, at the age of sixty-nine, and Jacqueline succumbed to Hodgkin's Lymphoma at her home in New York, May 1994, at the age of sixty-four.

John Kennedy's brother, 'Robert', was some years later, a leading Democratic candidate, nominated for the presidency. He was very popular with young voters, and especially the poorer African and Hispanic voters. After celebrating a major victory of the California primary, he, was hit three times when a Palestinian man opened fire, whilst leaving The Ambassador Hotel in Los Angeles in the early hours of 5th June 1968. Kennedy died the following day. A 24-year-old man, 'Sirhan Sirhan', was arrested and later sentenced to life imprisonment. His motive was because of America's support of Israel during the 1967 Six-Day War.

The Kennedy's were to suffer more drama during 1969, when Edward Kennedy, the youngest of the four brothers, who, at the time, was also in line to inherit John Kennedy's legendary presidency, only to see it dashed by what today is known as the Chappaquiddick Incident. It was late in the night of July 18, after leaving a cottage party, Senator Edward Kennedy plunged his car off a wooden bridge, on the small Massachusetts island of Chappaquiddick. The car landed upside-down in a tidal pond. Kennedy escaped the submerged vehicle, but his passenger, 28-year-old Mary Jo Kopechne, did not.

Instead of trying to save Mary Jo, get help, or immediately report the incident to the police, Kennedy left the scene of the incident and made it back to his motel. In an attempted to invent alibies, he complained to the hotel manager about a noisy party that was going on, ordered newspapers for the following day, took a shower and went to bed. It was not until he had spoken to a friend and two lawyers the following morning, he finally called the police to report the fatal accident. Which was, by then, ten hours later.

Divers from a local fire department were called to remove the body from the car, and said that if they had been summoned immediately, they would have possibly had time to pull out Mary Jo. She had not drowned but had survived in an air pocket inside the car for some time and was asphyxiated only when the oxygen ran out several hours later.

In a well-prepared televised speech one week later, Kennedy maintained that he had not been driving drunk at the time, and that there was no truth in immoral conduct. He attributed his actions to concussion, shock and confusion following the accident. In his statement to the police, he had stated that Mary Jo complained of feeling unwell during the party and he was heading to the ferry, taking her back to her hotel. However, the fact that she had left her purse and hotel keys back in the cottage gave doubt to this claim. One newspaper claimed that his weakness to chase vulnerable women had brought his dream of reaching the White House to a shameful end.

Timing was somewhat on Kennedy's side that weekend, as most Americans, together with the rest of the world, were glued to their TV sets, absorbed with the Moon Landing following the Apollo 11's lift off from Cape Canaveral on July 16th of that year.

The Vietnam War was a tumultuous time in American history and was covered daily by the news media from around 1965 onwards. The nation, at large, was divided on whether or not it should get involved in a conflict so far from home. Nevertheless, thousands of American soldiers fought and died in the war. And many more soldiers were taken prisoner by the Viet Cong. The news coverage, showing typical American warmongering and their patriotic heroes, gave the impression of glory and that victory would be imminent, but as time passed, the people realised they were not being told the truth, which led to an increase in public pressure to end the war. Many statements released about the military situation in Vietnam were simply untrue. Despite this, a silent majority still supported the war, even though they knew that involvement was a mistake and costing the lives of thousands of young men, only because an American military defeat, to them, was unthinkable. The peace movement that evolved in America during the mid-sixties, grew into a social movement, and later spread to Britain, as famous singers, rock bands, hippies and actors joined the students and mothers in demonstrating against the war. From where we stood, the war had an almost romantic or attractive feeling about it. Every night, we would watch news reals of villains and heroes, engaged in combat or soldiers on patrol in a picturesque terrain of green paddy fields and jungle, surrounded by mountains. Platoons of marine's with M3 machineguns slung over their shoulders, a cigarette in their mouths, bringing in Viet Cong prisoners they had captured. Fleets of helicopters flying in reinforcements and supplies. Elegant Vietnamese girls with beautiful smiles in their national dress, the *ao dai*, welcoming the soldiers. In the meantime, mass anti-war demonstrations and marches, in Washing DC and across the USA and other cities in the world, were escalating

I had no idea what the war was about, and at the time, I didn't really care. During that summer of 1965, still at the age of fourteen, I started my second job in the car factory, which I suppose, was the time I passed from boyhood to manhood. My wage packet at the end of each week was £3.00, which was reduced a few weeks later, on my fifteenth birthday, when income tax was deducted. We were paid in cash in small brown envelopes called wage packets at the end of each working week, and the first thing I did when I got home was pay my mother £1.00 board and lodging money. I learned how to work on the various machines and fabricate components. I spent time in the heat treatment shop, the assembly line and the inspection and quality control of parts. I enjoyed smelling of machine oil and arriving home tired at the end of the day. Some evenings, before going home, I would visit the factory's 'Working Man's Club', and sit with workers older than myself, drinking beer and smoking the cheapest Woodbine or Park Drive cigarettes. I would listen to their stories and disputes about football, politics and of course, the most interesting topic for a young man at that age, 'sex'! My work mates were of families from all over the UK and Ireland, both unselfish and generous, whether helping a young man to understand and carry out the work or providing him with a beer and a cigarette. However, being young, naive and a virgin, I had to put up with my fair share of banter such as – I was warned that excessive masturbating caused hairs to grow in the palm of the hand. I would sometimes check my palms when no one was looking. I can assure you now, however, that it does not. There was very little political correctness at that time. If you were fat, you would almost certainly be called a fat bastard and so on. The best Irish jokes were probably the ones told by the Irish themselves. By the time I was sixteen or seventeen, I could hold my own at darts, dominoes and snooker, and put away a few pints of beer. It was around this time, with money in my pocket and a group of new friends, I became part of the mod culture hanging around the pubs and nightspots around Coventry.

In the meantime, as the sixties rolled on, and I was enjoying my youth, young men my age in the USA were being drafted to fight in Vietnam and were losing theirs to the war. The atrocities of the war were now becoming apparent to all. That beautiful Vietnamese terrain became an inferno. It would sap the strength of the soldiers. Out on patrols, they were constantly wet through – sometimes it would rain for weeks on end, if not the rain, then the sweat from the extensive heat. They waded through paddy fields and slimy, infested swamps for hours, up to their knees in water or struggled through thick elephant grass up to their necks. They constantly had to remove leaches sucking blood from their bodies. They were given penicillin shots to help against the running sores and festering ulcers on their legs and feet. The mosquitoes were unbearable, but more unbearable was the constant threat of being ambushed, hit by a sniper's bullet, stepping on a land mine or falling into a booby trap, set with bamboo spikes, which happened all too often. The choppers, bringing out reinforcements to those holding strategic hillsides against the Viet Cong far out in the jungle, would load the bodies of dead soldiers in body bags to transport back to base, which was a chilling welcome for new young recruits to encounter when arriving on the same chopper, to commence their first assignment in the field. And those beautiful, smiling Vietnamese girls so often turned out to be Viet Cong informers. The war, as far as the top command were concerned, became a game of statistics, "*Yes, we lost five Marines during attacks on Hills 327 and 268 today, but we killed ten of theirs.*"

1.7 million young American men, age nineteen to twenty-five, were drafted from 1965 to 1973 to serve in the Vietnam War, to fight a war that many believe should never have happened. The majority of these were young men that came from unprivileged backgrounds; from the slums, of the lower class and the less educated areas – farmers, and construction workers, who were given no choice other than to be sent to prison if they did not sign up, whereas many from the wealthy and educated families received deferments and avoided the draft. The establishment that got involved in the war, and their elite friends, did not send their sons and daughters to fight, in fact, many of their sons and daughters became supporters of the anti-war movement. Latino and African American males were assigned to combat more regularly than drafted white Americans, however, once drafted, those with higher levels of education were often assigned to work in the back lines.

The US army were well equipped with fleets of helicopters, aircraft, tanks, amphibious troop carriers and communication equipment, which is fine if you know where and who the enemy are! The Vietnam War was not a conventional war; there were no front lines, they could make no strategic battle plans, unlike previous wars, and there were no battles as such. They thought the Vietnamese Army were simple peasants, trained to be guerrillas, but found that they were well trained, lethal and determined. They underestimated the determination of the Vietnamese people to rid themselves of an unwelcomed occupational force and were no match for their guerrilla-style tactics. As time went on, the fighting became more intense and the Americans were throwing everything they had at the enemy.

The Viet Cong were transporting manpower, arms and materials, along the Ho Chi Minh Trail from the north to support their colleagues in the south, known as the 'National Front for the Liberation of South Vietnam'. Named after the

North Vietnamese president Ho Chi Minh, the trail ran for approximately 1,000 kilometres across mountain ranges, primitive jungle and rain forests, in large parts passing through Laos and Cambodia. Reinforcements, together with hundreds of tons of equipment, were transported by hand, bicycle, ox cart, mules, and in places, by truck, The Ho Chi Minh Trail has been recorded as one of the great achievements of military engineering of the 20th century.

The CIA, without any support of the American people, went on to create a secret war against Laos to prevent the supplies moving south. Between 1964 and 1973, the peasants, farmers, and villagers living along the areas of the Ho Chi Minh Trail lived under a holocaust of US bombers. The US Air Force carried out more than 600,000 bombing missions against the country or one every nine minutes for ten years. A number of towns, namely Xieng Khouang, Ville Phonsavan and Khang Khay, were completely destroyed. More explosives were dropped on this small, poor country than by all sides during the whole of the Second World War. Nobody really knows how many Lao people lost their lives. The population of one whole village were killed in one instant, while sheltering in a cave, when an American pilot steered a phosphorus rocket direct into the mouth of the cave.

The United States military sprayed approximately 20,000,000 US gallons of '*Agent Orange*' over Vietnam, eastern Laos and parts of Cambodia. Agent Orange is a mixture of chemicals mixed with jet fuel. The goal was to destroy forests and rural land, depriving the enemy of cover, destroying crops and the ability of peasants to provide food for the Viet Cong guerrillas. It was later discovered that nearly all the food they were destroying, was being produced for the civilian population. In some areas, thousands of people were left malnourished and starving. It is estimated that 400,000 people were killed or maimed, and 500,000 children born with birth defects, and up to one million people are disabled or have health problems due to Agent Orange.

Flame throwers and bombs containing '*Napalm*', a substance of mixed plastic polystyrene, benzene and gasoline, that sticks to anything, and burns for up ten minutes up to a temperature of 2,000 degrees F, were used to eliminate enemy guerrilla fighters, destroy rural buildings, hamlets and villages. Napalm causes the most terrible pain imaginable and almost always results in the death to it victims.

The American soldiers began to make more enemies than friends amongst the South Vietnamese that they were there to protect. Many had long forgotten their purpose of protecting democracy and stopping communism. They were fighting for each other, for their own lives, or retaliation for their friends, who had been killed or maimed by the enemy. Innocent farmers and peasants, including women and children, were killed when their homes and villages were destroyed. Anyone suspected as being associated with the enemy was treated as such. Over a period of time, families and friends of innocent victims that were killed, disappeared or taken prisoner came to regard the Americans as the aggressors, resulting in thousands of South Vietnamese siding with and secretly supporting communists.

Horrific images of the war began to appear on the television news broadcasts every day, and the real cost to human life of soldiers from all sides and innocent civilians, was becoming apparent to the public. One particular revelation was that US soldiers slaughtered more than 400 unarmed civilians during an attack on their village. Knowing news of the massacre would cause a scandal, officers higher up in command immediately made efforts to downplay the bloodshed. The incident prompted global outrage when it became public knowledge the following year, in November 1969, when exposed by three US servicemen, who had tried to stop the massacre and rescue the hiding civilians.

The report of the My Lai massacre, on the morning of 16th March 1968, describes how an infantry division (Charlie Company 1st Battalion of the 11th Infantry Brigade) was dropped in to the South Vietnamese village of 'Son My', where it was suspected that there was a strong communist presence. Under the orders of the lieutenant, 347 unarmed villagers, consisting mainly of women and children, were massacred. Babies were shot, soldiers beat and raped women, before shooting them, and grenades killed those that were hiding in bomb shelters or trying to escape the carnage. All the houses were burned to the ground. If that wasn't enough, the soldiers shot the water buffaloes, pigs and chickens, and threw dead animals in the wells to poison the water. In total, over 500 people were killed at Son My, most in the Hamlet of My Lai, plus another 90 by another platoon near the same village. By the time the My Lai massacre ended, 504 people were dead. Amongst the victims were 182 women, seventeen of them pregnant and one hundred and seventy-three children, including fifty-six infants. More and more Americans and people from all over the world were turning against the war.

Direct US military involvement in Vietnam ended in August 1973, but the end of the war came on 30 April 1975, when Saigon (later renamed Ho Chi Minh City) fell to the North Vietnamese Army.

Ho Chi Minh, known to the people as 'Uncle Ho', was a very simple man, well-travelled, and, until this day, beloved and never forgotten by the Vietnamese people. He grew up a nationalist, to lead the country successfully to independence, first from the Japanese, the French, and later, the Americans. Ho was born May 19, 1890, in the village of Kim Lien, in Annam province, central Vietnam. In his early years, he worked for a short time as a teacher, before moving to Saigon, where he attended a course in navigation. In 1911, he found work as a kitchen hand on a French steamer which took him from Saigon to Marseilles, and then went on to London, where he spent two years before moving back to France in 1919. Later, he went to the US where he worked as a cook and a baker in New York and Boston.

In later years, after spending some time in a Hong Kong prison for being proclaimed as a political revolutionist, he travelled to Moscow, where he spent seven years studying and teaching at the Lenin Institute, followed by some years in China, serving as an adviser to the Chinese communists in the Sino-Japanese War. On returning, (after 30 years) and becoming president of North Vietnam, he led the struggle to reunite the north of the country with the south. He once explained, "*It was patriotism that inspired me, not communism*." The US, who opposed Ho Chi Minh, because he was a communist, completely underestimated his strengths, his support and the will of the Vietnamese people, from both the north and South of Vietnam, which led them to finally withdrawing from the country. 'Ho' died of heart failure, at the age of seventy-nine, in Hanoi, six years before reunification between the north and south was finally achieved.

The total number of deaths in the Vietnam War (1965 – 1974) was estimated at 1,350,000, being 282,000 US & allied troops, 627,000 (north and South civilian deaths), 444,000 VC military deaths.

Gary Lineker once said, "Football is a simple game. Twenty-two men chase a ball for ninety minutes, and, at the end, the Germans win!" Which is not altogether true. Ask any English man if England has ever won a football World Cup, and they will proudly say, "Yes, we beat West Germany in the 1966 World Cup Final." Ask them if they ever watched the game, most of them will probably say no, because more than fifty years have passed, and many would be too young to remember, or not even born at the time. Maybe, it's now the time for us England supporters to move on and surrender our glory to the history books. The national team has yet to reach the final of a major tournament, since they faced West Germany at Wembley Stadium in 1966, thus becoming international soccer's greatest underachievers. However, it is fair to say, that winning the World Cup back then, complemented the exhilaration and everything else that was happening around Britain during the mid-sixties.

Winning the 1966 World Cup at Wembley Stadium, on 30th July 1966, was one of the most celebrated events of the decade, and one that we can all remember where we were and what we were doing on that particular day and time.

I was on a bus with three of my friends, coming back from our summer holidays on the east coast of England. Many industrial cities had a dedicated period, each year, when they would shut down the factories for the workers' annual holidays. If I remember, 'The Coventry holiday fortnight' was the last two weeks of July. We had been to a small fishing town, called 'Wells Next the Sea', which was supposedly for one week, staying at a small guesthouse. It was the first time I went on a holiday without my parents. We were four young mods, wandering around Wells Next the Sea, like we owned the place, the in-crowd from the big city, we found a pub that would serve us beer, even though we were well below the legal drinking age of eighteen years, and we each managed to find ourselves a local girlfriend, we had a few purple heart pills in our pockets to complement our mod image. We were in our element!

When the day finally came to return home and catch a local bus along the coast to Cromer bus station, for our onward connection back to Coventry, we stood with our girlfriends, none of us happy to be leaving at the end of our holiday. We had enjoyed ourselves so much. After a small conference between ourselves regarding the amount of funds we had available between us, which wasn't much, and the pros and cons of whether to return home or not, one of the lads said, "Fuck it, let's just stay." So, for the second week, we slept under a Life Boat House on the beach, used the washroom facilities of a caravan site close by, and during the days, worked on a nearby farm, picking fruit, which earned us just enough money to buy fish and chips and a couple of beers in the evenings. It was during our coach journey back to Coventry, the World Cup was being played and each time a goal was scored, it was announced over the radio, to the excitement and cheers or jeers of the passengers.

When Bobby Moore, the England Captain, climbed the thirty nine steps to the Royal Box at Wembley, to receive the solid gold Jules Rimet trophy from Queen Elizabeth, you could say, he had 'Pickles' to thank for it, given that the trophy had been stolen while on exhibition at the Central Hall in Westminster London, just a couple of months before the start of the tournament.

Supposedly, the trophy was being guarded by two uniformed officers around the clock, plus two plainclothes officers during the day, when, on Sunday 20th March, whilst a Methodist service was being held in an adjoining hall, the trophy (valued at £30,000) disappeared. Someone had forced open the display case and the rear doors of the building and made off with it.

Police later gave a description of a suspicious-looking man, who was seen in the building at the time of the theft. He was described as, being in his early thirties, of average height with thin lips, greased black hair and a possible scar on his face. I have to agree that he would look like a suspicious character, under any circumstances!

Pickles, a mongrel dog that found the World Cup, became one of the star characters of the tournament, when, being taken for a walk, began sniffing at something that was laying under a hedge. His owner, David Corbett, went to see what it was, and found a parcel of old newspaper tied with string. When he opened the parcel, he recognised the trophy, when he noticed the previous world cup winner's names on the bottom. Pickles and the stolen World Cup became a bigger news story than everything else going on at the time, including a general election.

David Corbett received rewards, totalling £6,000, and, for a short time, he and Pickles became celebrities, appearing on TV and in some movies. Corbett also attended the players' celebration dinner after the World Cup Final.

Brazil were horrified, saying it was sacrilege that would never have been committed in Brazil, where even its thieves loved football too much. Ironically, Brazil won the following World Cup four years later in Mexico, and were allowed to keep the trophy, after winning the competition for a third time. But it was stolen again, in 1983, in Rio de Janeiro, and never recovered.

The 1966 tournament was not as well organised or had the media coverage and was much smaller than modern World Cups, with only sixteen teams competing.

Due to the FIFA qualifying format, which did not allow one African team a direct route to the finals, everyone from the African continent, thirty-one nations, decided to withdraw in protest. They felt teams winning their division should merit qualification to the finals. North Korea and Australia were the only teams from the Asian/Oceanic zone. North Korea became famous for their 1-0 victory over one of the favourites, Italy.

Not all the games were televised. For some reason, all the four quarter finals kicked off at the same time on a Saturday afternoon. One of the games, France v Uruguay which were in England's group, clashed with the regular Greyhound meeting also being held at Wembley Stadium, so 'of course' they couldn't disrupt the dog racing, so had to move the World Cup game to an alternative location.

Brazil were knocked out of the tournament at the group stage with Edson Arantes do Nascimento, Brazil's best player being kicked so much in their first game against Bulgaria. He was not fit to play in the 2nd game against Hungry. He appeared in the 3rd game, against Portugal, where he was heavily fouled, only to get up and be tackled harder again by the same Portuguese player. The German referee did not even caution the player concerned, and Edson played no further part in the game.

The South Americans claimed that the tournament was rigged by the Europeans and thought it no coincidence that English officials refereed two of Brazil's games and a German refereed England's bad-tempered game with Argentina. Due to the number of controversial incidents in this game and the England Manager Alf Ramsey referring to the Argentinians as 'animals', football rivalry between these two countries remains highly competitive until today. An English referee also refereed the German-Uruguay match, where two Uruguayans were sent off.

The World Cup Final, itself, had everything a cup final should have. Two teams, with some great players and evenly matched, goals, extra time and controversy. Two of the world's top players, Bobby Charlton and Germany's Franz

Beckenbauer, however, later admitted that they felt they didn't contribute as much as they would have liked to the game. Both their managers had given them the same instructions, "*Stay close to him, don't let him out of your sight*," so they spent most of the day looking at each other. Beckenbauer once said, that the most wonderful moment of the game was when the final whistle went, and he didn't have to follow Bobby around the Wembley pitch anymore. A crowd of over 97,000 were in Wembley Stadium to watch the game, but still there were 97 empty seats.

England won the toss, and Bobby Moore elected to kick off, but within twelve minutes West Germany were ahead, when some bad defending allowed Helmut Haller a shot on target and made it 1-0 to West Germany. A few minutes later, England won a free kick, which Moore took quickly, floating a cross into the West German area, where Geoff Hurst was waiting to level the scores with a downward glancing header. The teams went in level at half time.

The second half continued with the teams evenly balanced, when in the seventy-seventh minute, England won a corner. Alan Ball delivered the ball into the area, where Geoff Hurst's deflected shot found Martin Peters, who placed his shot past the German goalkeeper from eight yards out. 2-1 to England. The Germans pressed hard for an equaliser, and with the English fans celebrating and waiting for the referee to blow the final whistle, the Germans, being Germans, were not finished yet and, scored an equaliser in the eighty-ninth minute, forcing the game into extra time. 2-2.

England continued to be the aggressor during the first part of extra time. Bobby Charlton, with a shot that struck the post and another that went agonisingly wide. With eleven minutes gone, Geoff Hurst received a cross from Alan Ball, turned and shot from close range. The ball hit the underside of the cross bar, bounced down to the goal line, span out of the goal and was cleared by a German defender. The England players threw their arms in the air in celebration. The Germans ran to the referee, appealing that the ball had not crossed the line. The Swiss referee was uncertain and had to consult his linesman. Of course, the millions of English TV viewers were sure it was a goal, and the eagle-eyed Azerbaijan linesman, even though him and the referee did not understand or speak each other's language, with non-verbal communication indicated that it was. The referee awarded the goal which has remained controversial ever since.

During the second part of extra time, the Germans pushed hard, desperate to score an equaliser. Supporters were on the edge of the field, waiting to run on and celebrate when with one minute to go, Bobby Moore found Geoff Hurst with a long pass. Hurst carried the ball forward just as the TV commentator, Kenneth Wolstenholme, was saying, *"And here comes Hurst, he's got some people on the pitch, they think it's all over."* Hurst hit a tremendous shot, hitting the back of the net, giving the German goalkeeper no chance, "*It is now, it's four*!" Which some consider to be one of the most famous sayings in English football.

We can proudly boast that, until this day, Geoff Hurst is the only player ever to score a hat trick in a World Cup Final.

Traditionally, when a player scores a hat trick, he gets to keep the match ball as a souvenir, which was not the case for Geoff Hurst. After the game, Hurst sat waiting for the ball to appear, or someone to arrive and present him with it. But it didn't happen. The German player Helmut Haller, who scored the first German goal in the final, took it home with him and stored it in his loft. It was only thirty years later, after campaigns from two British tabloid newspapers, it was returned to its rightful owner. A newspaper headline read '*They think it's all over...it's his now. The Daily Mirror gets Geoff his ball back.*'

Oh, by the way, Edson Arantes do Nascimento, 'Pele', is the only player to win three World Cup Medals. He played for the Brazilian club Santos and was part of the Brazilian national teams that won three World Cup finals of 1958, 1962, and 1970. Pele was only seventeen years of age when he scored two goals in the final, when Brazil defeated Sweden 5-2, having scored a hat trick against France in the semi-final. Pele holds the Guinness World Record for goals scored during his career, with a total of 1,281 goals in 1,363 games (including unofficial friendlies). In 1967, Santos Football Club went to play in Africa, in what was then the Congo. There was a civil war going on at the time, but after a meeting between government leaders and the rebels, a forty-eight-hour ceasefire was agreed so the game could go ahead and people could watch their idol Pele.

Pele did get sent off once in his career, which resulted in thousands of fans rioting in the stadium. The game was suspended, while the officials discussed the situation. The result was, the referee sent himself off and was replaced by a linesman. Pele finished his career playing in the USA for the New York Cosmos. In 1994, Pele was appointed a UNESCO Goodwill Ambassador and, during 1997, at a ceremony in Buckingham Palace, received an honorary knighthood from Queen Elizabeth II. On meeting President Reagan, the president introduced himself by saying, "*Hi, my name is Ronald Reagan, I'm the President of the United States of America. But you don't need to introduce yourself, because everyone knows who Pele is!*"

A footballing genius, and considered as one of the best players in the world during the sixties' decade, who sadly never had the opportunity to shine on the world stage (in spite of winning thirty-seven caps with his country), was a shy young Irishman from Belfast, by the name of George Best. Best joined Manchester United, turning professional on his seventeenth birthday, in May 1963, and made his debut in September, helping them to win the league title in his second season, and another during the 1966-67 season. Best was named European Footballer of the Year in 1968, and was instrumental in United's European Cup glory when they beat Benfica 4-1 at Wembley, after extra time, having eliminated Benfica (one of Europe's top clubs at that time) from the same tournament, with two goals the year before.

Best was a naturally gifted player, beautiful to watch – he was fast, he could dribble, he would ride tackles, brush past players and leave defenders in his wake. He would score from any angle. At that time, the pitches were not maintained as they are today, the referees less protective and the defenders more aggressive. Unlike many players today, Best took everything they threw at him, did not dive looking for free kicks and rarely retaliated.

At the prime of his career in 1974, he unexpectedly quit United at the age of twenty-seven. One of his complaints was that the club were not building a future around himself and the younger players, and so were underperforming, leading to them being relegated that 1973-74 season. I watched Best play a number of times and can happily boast that I went to watch Coventry play United at Old Trafford that season and we won 3-2, to help them on their way.

George Best also became a fashionably celebrity outside the game, with his long hair, good looks and playboy image, earning him the name, 'the Fifth Beatle', a footballing product of the sixties' revolution. Just as the bands and film stars had young female groupies, so did George. Young girls would attend the matches just to get a sight of him, shrieking whenever he was on the ball, whilst groans of anxiety from the opposing supporters could be heard, worrying what he was going to do with it. Sadly, the fortune and fame came too soon, and brought with it a serious drinking problem, which he nurtured for most of his life. Being a modest and shy person, the drink gave him confidence. He went on to play for a number of unfashionable, professional and amateur football clubs around the world, but his dependency on alcohol affected his ability to perform. Even so, smaller clubs that normally attracted 7 to 10,000 supporters were getting as many as 20,000 when Best was playing. He finally retired from playing (thought, by many, a squandered talent) at the age of thirty-seven in 1984.

Best died at the age of fifty-nine in London, during November 2005, due to complications and having not fully recovering from liver transplant surgery two years earlier.

A quote from Best, "*In 1969, I gave up women and alcohol. It was the worst twenty minutes of my life*."

Throughout the 1960s, the USA and the Soviet Union were involved in a 'Cold War'. They did not go in to battle with each other, but there was a continuous tension between the two powers, their politics and their respective allies. They fought each other indirectly by spying and backing opposite sides in other countries wars. The Cold War was a result of mistrust of different political systems and the disagreement over the rebuilding of Germany and Europe.

The 'Space Race' became another way for the two powers to compete against each other; to obtain supremacy in space and to show to the world which country had the best science, technology and power. The Soviet Union are considered to have started the so-called space race, in October 1957, when they successfully launched Sputnik 1, the first earth satellite in history, and lead the race in the early years. A month later, they launched Sputnik 2, which was the first spacecraft to carry an animal into orbit, a stray dog named *Kudryavaka* ('Curly'), but later known to the world as *Laika* ('Barker'). Years later, it was revealed that Laika only lived for a few hours, before dying of overheating inside her capsule. Poor Laiker. In spite of her fame as being the first dog in space, she became a stray dog there too. In 1960, Sputnik 5 carried two dogs into orbit that, after seventeen orbits, were successfully recovered on its return to earth. Despite the Cold War tensions, the following year, the Soviet leader, Khruschev, gave a puppy (with a little Soviet Passport) of one of the dogs to Kennedy's daughter Carolina. The dog, known as Pushinka, eventually gave birth to four puppies of her own, which President J. Kennedy referred to as his 'pupniks'.

Someone later remarked that it was just as well that the dogs returned and were not intercepted and interrogated by aliens. They would have been baffled as to how these four-legged hairy creatures, with a limited vocabulary of a few growls and barks, that licked their genitals and sniffed each other's back ends, had the technology to find their way into space. They would definitely have a strange perception of us earthlings.

The Soviets intensified their space programme over the next three years with a number of successful missions, including Luna 3, which orbited the Moon and photographed seventy percent of the its surface, and during April 1961, the USSR went on to take a clear lead by sending the first man into space, and the first man to orbit the Earth. 'Yuri Gagarin' commented on his return, quote, "Orbiting Earth in the spaceship, I saw how beautiful our planet is. People, let us preserve and increase this beauty, not destroy it!" I wonder what the world's most famous astronaut would think today if he saw how we are slowly destroying our beautiful planet! In June 1963, the USSR sent the first woman into space, 'Valentina Tereshkova', who also became the first civilian, as she was not a professional astronaut, but an ordinary cotton mill worker. This astonished many, given that the space programmes of both sides were predominantly male dominated. Two years later, a Soviet cosmonaut, 'Alexei Leonov', performed the first spacewalk in history when he spent twelve minutes outside his spacecraft. He almost didn't get back inside, when he found his spacesuit had over pressurised and would not fit through the hatch. Only when he released excess air, was he able to get back inside. In 1966, the Soviet Luna 9 became the first spacecraft to soft land on the Moon.

1967 was a bad year for both sides, when, in January, three American astronauts, Gus Grissom, Ed White and Roger Chaffee, lost their lives when fire broke out in their Apollo 1 capsule, whilst carrying out tests on the launch pad. A few months later, a Soviet cosmonaut was killed when the parachutes of his Soyuz 1 capsule failed to open on re-entry. There were a number of other fatalities that happened during spaceflight training or testing programmes.

So, who won the space race? To some the answer is very clear. The Soviets won, especially when their early achievements are considered. They launched the first Satellite, first animal, first man, first woman, first spacewalk and first space station. The man behind all this, the chief designer, working with what can only be described as a paltry budget, was a genius engineer by the name of 'Sergei Korolev'. Unlike the Americans, the Soviet Union did not have a single space agency like NASA, which, following

Kennedy's vision of putting a man on the Moon, had unwavering support and funding from the US Government.

After years of Soviet space dominance, the USA took the lead and made history by putting the first man on the Moon. A Moon landing had been the stuff of science-fiction. Just a few years previously, until the Apollo II Mission, when on July 20th 1969, millions of people from all over the world watched with mixed emotions, fascination, pride and fear as Neil Armstrong and Buzz Aldrin landed their lunar module, the Eagle, on the lunar surface to become the first men to walk on the Moon. In the meantime, a third astronaut Michael Collins, remained on board the command module, 'Columbia', orbiting the Moon.

It is debatable whether the Moon landing was humanity's greatest accomplishment ever, as some will argue that the invention of television, the internet or the progress of medicines are greater achievements to benefit mankind, than landing on a worthless hunk of rock in space. It was, however, a major landmark, and the most extraordinary in history, and a remarkable way to draw the curtain on the sixties' decade.

My memory of the Moon landing is a little blurred, as all three UK television channels, BBC1, BB2 and ITVs coverage of the Apollo II Mission went on for a number of days, from the launching on 16th July, until the astronauts returned safely to Earth on 24th July.

Watching the actual landing, was both a little tense and boring, as everything happened so slowly. The quality of the sound and the pictures was, at times, very poor. I remember the sound of audible bleeps when the crew of the landing module, '*Eagle*', were communicating with the Houston NASA mission control, and when, apparently with only thirty seconds of fuel remaining on board, the module finally settled on the Moon's surface, and some audible bleeps, before informing mission control, "*Houston, tranquillity base here, the Eagle has landed.*" The response was, "*Bleep-bleep, we copy you, you've got a bunch of guys on the ground, about to turn blue, we are breathing again.*" We then waited for around twenty minutes for the hatch to open and Neil

Armstrong, slowly climbed out of the module, down the ladder, jumped on to the surface and said to an estimated 600 million viewers worldwide, "*That's one small step for man, one giant leap for mankind.*"

The first images we saw, as Neil Armstrong half-stepped and half-floated across the Luna surface, was a desolate landscape, with no clouds or trees or anything that resembled life of any kind.

Buzz Aldrin joined Armstrong some minutes later and, together, they set about planting the American flag, setting up equipment, taking photographs, collecting data and rock samples, before returning to Eagle two hours later. The following morning, the Eagle rendezvoused with Columbia, and after transferring all the data, equipment and Moon rocks, was jettisoned into space, and the three astronauts began their flight back to earth, aboard Columbia. Eight days, three hours and 18 minutes after lift-off, the astronauts landed in the Pacific Ocean and were put into quarantine aboard the USS Ship Hornet, before landing in Hawaii.

Before leaving Hawaii, the famous astronauts were required to fill in a customs declaration form. In the section asking arrival /departure from, they had to write 'The Moon'.

However, the theory that the Moon landing was a deception has grown in popularity over the years, and it is estimated that more than 20% of Americans believe the US Government hoaxed the whole thing to assert their victory in the space race over Russia. Conspiracy theorists claim there are too many inconsistences evident, during the first Moon landing shown on live television.

Viewers noted that the American flag could be seen fluttering after the two astronauts placed it, the theory being that there is no air in the Moon's atmosphere, and therefore, no wind. There are no clouds on the Moon, and therefore, stars should have been visible, which should show brighter than what we see, through the Earth's atmosphere. On one photo, a rock in the foreground has the letter 'C' marked in it, which looks unnatural and is suggested to be a location marker for a film crew, and that the whole thing was filmed in the Nevada Desert!

Sometime later, photographs from the Apollo 15 mission appeared, having clearly the identical backdrop of hills in the background, even though they were supposed to have been taken miles apart.

A number of tapes that contained original footage from the Apollo 11 moonwalk have since disappeared, with NASA claiming they might have been destroyed at a time when they were erasing old tapes to reuse to record satellite data!

The Moon Landing, fake news or what? Even if it was fake, I don't believe the Moon is made of cheese!

A few months before the Moon landing, a joint venture between Britain and France presented to the world the most exciting and beautiful commercial aircraft ever to take to the skies, when, on 2nd March 1969, Concorde 001 made its first test flight over Toulouse France, and later, the UK-built Concorde flew on April 9th. The aircraft first went supersonic on 01 October, that same year.

The Concorde was not just a plane, it was a symbol of the advanced technology and building skills we had in the UK, all those decades ago, an aviation achievement that the Americans nor the Russians could match, it was ,in a way, our space programme, ending the sixties' decade on a note of optimism, with dreams of bigger and better things to come. Even today, the Concorde, with its spectacular design and beauty, has an appearance far ahead of its time, or of something from the distant future, and has been ranked as the most beautiful jet airliner of all time. The name Concorde stands for harmony or union and was chosen to reflect the affiliation on the project between the United Kingdom and France.

Concorde was the first supersonic passenger airliner to enter service in 1976, bringing astounding new technologies to commercial aviation. It had a maximum speed of over twice the speed of sound at Mach 2.04 (1,354 mph or 2,180 km/hr), at an altitude of 60,000 ft., a height where passengers were able to see the curvature of the earth. Due to the intense heat, the aircraft would expand during flight by anywhere between six to ten inches. The nose was so long and pointed that it needed to be lowered during take-off and landing, so the pilots could see the runway and where they were going. In 1983, a British Airways Concorde flight set a New York to London record of two hours and fifty-six minutes.

However, Concorde was not the first commercial aircraft to fly supersonic, as two months before the first flight of Concorde, the Russian-built Tupolev TU-144 made its first test flight, and later went supersonic, when on. 26 May 1970, it became the first commercial transport to exceed Mach 2. However, its reputation and development programme were seriously damaged at the 1973 Paris Air Show. There was serious competition between the two airliners at that time, and the Soviet pilot bragged that he would outperform the Concorde. "*Just wait until you see us fly*," he said. "*Then you will see something*." Well we did. The plane crashed, killing all six of the crew and eight people on the ground.

Because of budget restrictions delaying further development, the plane was only introduced into passenger service on November 1977, two years after Concorde, but was grounded in 1978, after an improved version, TU-144D, crashed during a test flight prior to delivery. The TU-144 achieved only fifty-five scheduled flights.

There is some question as to whether Concorde, during its short life span, was a money-maker for the airlines. BA and Air France will say it was, however, it is said that operating costs were heavily subsidised by the British and French Governments. The aircraft was designed mainly for the transatlantic service between London, Paris and New York, but was so long in the development stage, it became somewhat obsolescent by the time it entered service. Concorde was most suited for business travellers, and the young jet set, celebrities with unlimited expense accounts that grew during the sixties. As time passed, more tourists and small business passengers began travelling by air, who were not prepared to pay twice the cost of a first-class fare, in order to arrive at their destination a couple of hours earlier.

Concorde had put prestige over efficiency, and eventually, it became evident that no airline in the world could ever make their operations profitable. Its only advantage was speed.

Phil Collins (of the band Genesis) drew a lot of attention in the summer of 1985, when he played two 'Live Aid Concerts' on both sides of the Atlantic on the same day. After finishing his gig at the Wembley Stadium, a helicopter flew him to Heathrow Airport and he flew supersonic on Concorde to New York, where a Helicopter was waiting to delivery him to the concert at Philadelphia.

Ironically, if Concorde had been released for commercial service some years earlier, a number of airlines would have placed orders – those that did, cancelled them after the stock market crash in 1973 and the oil crises a year earlier. The British and French hoped to sell hundreds, but in the end, only sixteen were built. They were used by British Airways and Air France. Passenger to fuel ratio was just not viable. Concorde used roughly 25,629 litres per hour on an average length of a flight of 3 1/2 hours. So, in total a Concorde flight, with a maximum of only 100 people, used 89,708 litres of jet fuel. So, to compare Concorde to its transatlantic rival, the Boeing 747. A non-Concorde flight with a minimum of 400 passengers consumed 59,500 litres of fuel. So, Concorde, apart from the time, difference, flew far fewer people and consumed far more fuel. Another obstacle was the 'subsonic boom' (where it was claimed would disrupt people down below), which, only after some time, and a number of legal battles in US courts. was allowed to land in New York. The truth is, that opposition to Concorde on grounds of noise pollution had been encouraged by the United States Government, only because it lacked its own competitor and a commercial aircraft so advanced, in spite of generous funding to Boeing and Lockheed by the US Government.

There were numerous reasons why the Concorde was finally taken out of service, but the Air France crash of 25th July 2,000, was thought to be the beginning of the end. Air France Flight 4590, after departing from Paris-Charles de Gaulle, en-route to John F. Kennedy International Airport,

New York City, crashed, killing all 100 passengers and nine crewmembers on board, and four people on the ground.

It was the only fatal accident involving Concorde in its twenty-seven years of service, and the crash was not as a result of any defect of the aircraft or by its crew. According to the official investigation that followed, the disaster was caused by a metallic strip that had fallen from a Continental Airlines DC-10, which had taken off a few minutes before Concorde. It was found that a metal strip that had fallen from the airliner, punctured a tyre on Concorde's left main wheel bogie, during take-off. The tyre exploded, and a piece of rubber hit the fuel tank, which caused a fuel leak and led to a fire and engine failure, causing the aircraft to crash into a hotel in nearby Gonesse, two minutes after take-off. Before this incident, the Concorde was considered one of the safest planes in the world. The crash was, however, a convenient excuse by the airlines to retire the aircraft and reduce operating costs.

The Concorde made its final commercial flight, BA 002, from JFK, New York, to London, Heathrow, on Friday October 24th, 2003. A sad day, not only for aviation, but also for mankind. Jeremy Clerkson said, as he disembarked, "One small step for man, one giant step backwards for mankind."

Just as the Concorde had that exotic nostalgic vibe of the sixties, then so did the '*Jaguar E-Type*' sports car, with its advanced technology and timeless design. Its combination of beauty, high performance, and competitive pricing established the model as an icon of the motoring world.

It is difficult to describe what affect this British machine, designed and built in my hometown of Coventry, had, when it was launched in March 1961, at the Geneva Motor Show. It attracted the attention of the whole motoring world as no car had ever before. The Italians, who were known at the time for producing the most beautiful cars in the world, were struck dumb with astonishment. It had a list price of around £2,200, half the price of its more exotic rivals, and a speed of 150 mph, at a time the average family car could only achieve 70 mph. Neither an Aston Martin or Ferrari could match the E-Type's top speed, so it was no wonder that customer interest at the show was high, and by stealing the show, it made the headlines of motoring magazines the world over.

The car was designed by a wartime aircraft engineer, by the name of Malcom Sayer, considered to be one of the first engineers to apply the principles of aircraft streamline aero design to cars. He went on to spend twenty years of his life working for Jaguar. Production of the E-Type Jaguar came to an end during 1975. The last fifty to come off the line were black, each with a commemorative plaque, signed by Sir William Lyons, a co-founder of Jaguar cars. The car is just another legend of the sixties' era, and widely recognised as the most memorable car of the last century.

Both my father and I had a connection with Jaguar cars at that time, but for entirely different reasons. My father worked nights in the factory, as a maintenance electrician for nearly twenty years, whereas I made headlines in the local newspaper for bringing production to a standstill.

It happened one night, just before 5th November (bonfire night, 1963). I must have been thirteen at the time. We had been hanging around, looking to get into mischief, in the back lanes in an area close behind the Jaguar Browns Lane factory. Earlier, we had been chatting with a somewhat goofy, dumb and strangely, eccentric postman, who often rode his bike around the area in the evenings and stopped to chat with us boys. That particular evening, one of the lads asked if we could borrow some money from him, to which he kindly obliged. So, off we went to a shop, and bought some fireworks.

In a field behind the factory, there was a large concrete block, housing three cast iron manhole covers, a couple of meters above a large drainpipe that ran under a field into to a river some distance away. We found that if we dropped fireworks through the manhole covers into the drain below, the sounds of the exploding fireworks were amplified and echoed loudly along the pipe below. A strong smell of petrol was noticed when the manhole covers were opened, but we carried on regardless. *Anyway,* we thought. *Who cares? Something very exciting might happen.* Well, it did! There was an enormous explosion. The concrete slab, which must have weighed three or four tons, shifted its position. The manhole covers and us boys all flew high into the air, landing a fair distance away. It took some time for us to understand what exactly had just happened. Slowly, each one of us got to his feet, examining ourselves and were surprised to be in one piece, except for some singed hair and eyebrows, and tattered clothes, all caused from the heat and the blast.

We stood around, all totally speechless, for a while until one of the boys shouted, "Holy shit! Run for it!" In the meantime, the Jaguar factory completely blacked out, and we learned later that the assembly line ground to a halt, and cracks appeared in the concrete above the drainpipe leading out from the factory.

It only took the police around fifteen minutes to catch us, as we were running away down a back lane, when a police car appeared from the opposite direction. The police took us to a local hospital for medical examination, before interrogating us one by one and delivering us back to our homes.

My father, as I mentioned, was working nights and was in the factory at the time. He was not a happy man when he arrived home that morning, and immediately started complaining to my mother about 'some stupid little bastards', who had disrupted the production line at the factory, and all the work that they had to undertake that night in order to get the factory back to working status once again. He blamed it on their stupid parents, who obviously did not know how to discipline their kids and allowed them to hang around the streets at night. My mother told him to sit down, made him a mug of tea and said to him, "When you have finished your tea, I think you should go upstairs and have a word with your son."

It was the following evening, when my friend's sister, who was delivering papers, shouted across the road at me, and said, "Martin, you are in the paper." The headline read, '*Coventry School Boys Blow-up Jaguar Works*'. I was hoping that she was impressed, as I fancied her like mad and it certainly enhanced my rogue status at school.

Another car, which can only be described as an icon of the 1960s culture, as simple as it was at the time it was launched, is the Morris Mini Minor! The Mini was a car made for the masses. Modest as it was, it was affordable, and meant everything to a young adult owning their very first car. It was a special car, if only for its individuality.

The Mini was first launched in 1959, and unlike the E-Type Jaguar, the public were more baffled and somewhat amused, at what they saw, they never imagined a car design anything like it. But, of course, this was the sixties. The Mini came about for two reasons, one because of fuel shortage and price hikes, as a result of the Suez Crisis, during the late 1950s, which caused a slump in the sales of large cars, and two, because of Lenard Lord, head of BMC (British Motor Corporation), at the time's hatred of the small Italian Fiat and German Bubble cars, that were becoming popular in the UK. He vowed to design a proper miniature car that would outplace these. Alec Issigonis (later '*Sir Alec*'), an ex-Alvis employee was hired to implement Lenard Lord's ideas. He came up with a design that (he first sketched out on a tablecloth) and revolutionised the small car industry, by maximising the interior space, while shrinking all components. Issigonis insisted that the car would seat four, and no less than 80% of the car's volume be designated for passengers and their luggage. To achieve this, he utilised a front wheel drive with a transverse engine.

That little car that baffled and amused those that saw, if for the first time, went on to become the best-selling British car in history, selling close to 6 million units worldwide. The Mini, in spite of the various models and developments over the years, never lost its charm. To name a few there is the Clubman, the Pickup Truck the Mini Cooper, the Mini Cooper S, that amongst the many races and the rallies it won, went on to win the Monte Carlo Rally on three occasions in 1964, 65 & 67, and how can we forget the Mini Moke, which was originally designed as a military vehicle.

A few of my friends owned Mini's in the 1960s, and I can ensure that the car designed to seat four persons could easily accommodate six or seven young men on a night out, in and around Coventry or sharing the cost of the petrol on our annual trips to the coast. The Guinness World Record for persons squeezing into a classic Mini stand at twenty-three women.

Regarding sex in a Mini, you would have to refer the website, '*How to Have Sex in a Mini*', which advises, "*Obviously you have to have yourself and a Mini, next on the list you need a willing partner and a dark lane. Move front seat forward. Lower back rest not all the way...*" I will leave you to research the rest.

Chapter 15
Summer Holidays

Time you enjoyed wasting, was not wasted.

John Lennon.

I have not had a chilly windy beach holiday in the UK for as long as I can remember. There are many things that trigger memories and take us back to the past and places we have visited, they can be smell, taste, sounds, and even people. Thoughts of my summer holidays bring memories of caravan sites, beach huts, B&B, amusement arcades, donkey rides, sunburn, rainy days, buckets and spades, postcards, deck chairs, wind breaks, fish & chips, cockles and mussels, crabs, a windswept beach and the smell of salty seaweed and a happy family appreciating every minute.

I would think, that the beach today is one of the few places where young kids can be kids, just like we were, and forget about their iPads, mobile phones, and gadgets, and enjoy what we experienced when we were young – fun and adventure of the Great British Holiday. Over the years, I have visited many countries and exotic interesting places, Copacabana and Corcovado, The Table Top Mountain, Angkor Wat, The Plane of Jars, The Mekong and Amazon rivers, Hollywood, to name a few. But none of these ever excited me like the sights, sounds, smells and the sight of the blue/grey sea, stretching far out to the horizon, that came into view at the times we arrived from the midlands, as kids for our summer holidays, at some south or east coast English seaside resort.

In the early sixties, our family of five and the dog would arrive to take our annual holiday at some camp or caravan site, and sleep in my dad's van for a couple of nights, until our parents could find a suitable caravan or B&B that would suit their modest budget. A bread and breakfast was not always a good option, as many grumpy, old landladies would demand that guests had to stay outside between 10:00 am and 06:00 pm, which was a challenge for families with kids if it rained all day. Which it so often does in Britain.

Towards the end of the sixties, many caravan sites were upgraded with better facilities, and options of bars and restaurants on site. Owning a caravan became a working-class status symbol for some, even though the caravans were parked in the street, outside homes, for most of the year. Towing these things, and manoeuvring slowly around narrow country lanes in a family car was not an easy mission and getting stuck behind them for long periods, frustrating. It would turn drivers like my father into '*Incredible Green Hulks*', and incite language, us kids sitting in the back of the vehicle, didn't know existed, but knew we shouldn't imitate or try to repeat.

The sixties became the golden age of holiday camps, such as Butlins or Pontins, which provided cheap all-in holidays and innocent fun for the working class and their families. The camps were run almost military style, with PA systems sounding off to inform guests of mealtimes, or the time they should return to their chalets after an evening's entertainment. In the mornings, the camp was woken over the sound system with the legendry, *"Good Morning Campers,"* followed by the sounds of the Trebletones, with songs such as *'Morning*'. It went something like, *"Good morning, good morning another lovely day, even if it's wet, it's fine at Butlins, we won't let it spoil your holiday..."* The wooden chalets were small and in rows, which camp security would patrol during the hours of darkness, to ensure that everyone was tucked in asleep, and not sneaking into one another's chalets for a drinking session or a quick shag. The camps somewhat resembling a remand centre. Some camps, at their peak, would entertain as many 2,000 holidaymakers at one time. Holiday camps provided wholesome fun for all the family but were not for everyone. They tended to be a family tradition.

If you were looking for a peaceful holiday, you were in the wrong place.

In spite of all the innocent family fun that went on between the families, it is known that camp organisers, famously known as Redcoats (at Pontins they were known as Bluecoats), welcomed singles as holiday guests too, so that they and the camp entertainers got to enjoy their own seedy entertainment during their time off. Some of those that worked in the holiday camps, back then, have since described them as giant knocking shops.

There were strict rules. Kids back in the chalet by 07.30 pm. Redcoats would patrol during the evenings to keep an eye on the kids, whilst parents were watching a show or having a drink in the bar. Lights out at 10.30, no bad language or drunkenness, dress codes, males not to visit single ladies' chalets.

Families were encouraged to participate in all the activities and were not allowed back in their chalets between breakfast and lunch times. Family entertainment, or some activity, was arranged or available for all members of the family all day, from morning until the good night singalong. The activities consisted of anything they could invent. Trophies were given for knobbiest knee competitions, the prettiest baby, the glamorous granny, the best dad in drag. Families were pitted against each other, with games such as the egg and spoon race, husband and wife or kids three-legged race, the fastest dad. The camp PA system would inform what competitions were going on, and where and give instructions to those family members that should attend, wives only, children below ten years and so on.

Archives show wonderful photographs from the sixties, of holidaymakers having innocent fun in the camps during their holidays. One photo that comes to mind is of the 'Human Pyramid'. How many kids can you get on a lifeguard tower? The human pyramid is made up of as many kids as possible that can fit on a wooden tower, normally used by lifeguards to watch over swimmers at sea. The tower is a pedestal of three levels, thirty to forty feet in height. In the photo, there must be as many as forty kids on it at the different levels, some youngsters waving from the very top, others hanging from the sides. Those paranoid health and safety departments of today would have nightmares if they saw it. Not a safety harness or hardhat in sight, just a bunch of happy smiling faces.

The camps that exist today resemble holiday resorts. Gone are the chalets, smelling of cigarette smoke with shabby carpets in regimental rows. Improvements had to be made, as towards the late 1960s, the camps and the great British Beach Holidays were being overtaken by the coming of the Jet Age, which led to cheap package holidays to Spain and beyond, that provided flights, transfers and accommodation, combined with organised tours. These appealed more to those adults who had a sense of adventure and those looking for guaranteed sunshine. How cool it was at that time to be back in the local pub at home with a Mediterranean suntan and a new vocabulary.

"Give me a *Cuba Libre*."

"Sorry, what did you say?"

"Woops, sorry mate I just got back from Spain, I meant a rum and coke."

Overheard by another at the bar,

"Where did you go in Spain?"

"We were in Ibiza but went to Benidorm last year."

"Hmm, those places are okay but a bit touristy, we prefer *Cala Mesquida Majorca* now or *Lloret de Mar* on the *Costa Brava*."

"Yeah, well, we just go for the night life, cheap booze and to get fucked up."

And so, the verbal sparring goes on…

The Lord Mayer of one Spanish Holiday Resort was once asked what he thought of the British holidaymakers that were taking over his town. His reply was that he can't complain because they spend a lot of money and create jobs, but he couldn't understand the culture of the younger generation, and why they liked to get drunk and rowdy every night, and on the way home, do things like (Moonies) pulling their pants down and showing their bare asses to passing cars or others across the street!

A building boom was created at most Spanish resorts, catering for the European tourists. This was a period of many horror stories, where guests would arrive only to be told that the beautiful hotel with a sea view they had seen on the holiday brochure and booked back in Birmingham, was still under construction, but not to worry as the local agent had arranged rooms elsewhere. Guests were often relocated a good walk from the beach, with a room looking out over some wasteland, towards the back of town.

"So where is the restaurant?"

"*Nao problema mio amigo, manten la calma*, we have arranged for you to use the restaurant at the hotel along the road."

The hotel meals were very basic, normally paella or spaghetti with every meal, although some bars and restaurants realised that the Brits do like their home comforts and advertised the full English breakfast, fish & chips and pots of tea, etc. For many British working-class tourists, it was the first time they had been in the company of foreigners, flown on an airplane and tasted foreign food, or taken a shower instead of a bath, for that matter, Those seasoned visitors that had been before, could be seen proudly carrying the Robertson's marmalade, marmite or HP sauce that they had brought on holiday with them into the restaurant. The Spanish waiters were a novelty, especially to the young ladies, who found them very attractive. They were, however, from the poorer rural villages and did not speak English.

"Waiter, please I need a knife and fork."

"Si si."

Some minutes later,

"Waiter, please, por favor, I asked for a knife and fork."

"Si si."

Many more minutes later, get the attention of another waiter, "Waiter, I asked your amigo to get me a knife and fork." Looking at the plate of food and gesturing with the hands!

"Si, si."

"Shit, where did I see that place with the fish & chip sign?"

Mealtimes were set and the restaurants busy, they served one table at a time, and there were dozens of tables. Service was very slow. These guys had no sense of urgency.

Certain parts of the poolside and beach areas became national property, basically the Froggies, Krauts or Brits would stay close to their own. The Germans would piss everybody off by sneaking down to the pool early before breakfast and place their beach towels over the back of the sunbeds and deck chairs, therefore reserving their place in prime locations before the crowd arrived after breakfast. They still have this habit today.

This was an era when tour operators, such as Thomas Cook and Horizon Holidays, became big business and the smaller airports, such as Luton, East Midlands and Stanstead, sprang to life in support of the newly-formed budget airlines. The airports arrival and departure lounges were amusing places and a little unruly. The passengers would arrive from Spain, and afar in good spirits tanned and/or sunburned, with their duty-free bottles of wine, spirits and cigarettes, sombrero hats, and Spanish souvenirs of castanets, fans and flamenco dresses. Whilst those departing for their first overseas holiday, white and looking very apprehensive.

It was a novelty, and not uncommon during that time for families on their Sunday afternoon to pack a flask and some sandwiches, and drive to their nearest airport to spend the afternoon, sitting on the grass or in the car just to watch the planes come in to land or take off.

It was, I believe the summer of 1970, when the lads and I decided to go to Spain for our holidays and show them some British culture. We flew out of Birmingham Airport to Palma Majorca on, I don't know, maybe a DC-3 or DC-6 or could it have been a Boeing? (Even after a lifetime of flying, I don't have a habit of looking at what type of plane it is). Flying was more comfortable back then – no security checks, more legroom and fewer delays. Although, the planes were noisier inside the cabin and take off not so smooth. There was also a lingering smell of cigarettes, as smoking was allowed for passengers seated towards the rear of the plane. It is hard to believe now, that after take-off and the no-smoking lights were switched off, a good number of passengers would light-up their cigarettes at the same time!

It was our first experience of flying and my friend, sitting next to me, was nervous at the best of times. Shortly after boarding and waiting to start the engines, we saw the pilot appear out of the cockpit and start chatting with one off the airport ground staff. Silence, then my friend remarks…

"That's the pilot, he looks worried."

"He looks okay to me."

"No, look at his face he's explaining something to that guy. Could be a problem."

Silence, then…

"There have been two in the last few weeks."

"Two what?"

"Plane crashes, they come in threes you know."

Later, taxying out to the runway,

"Holy shit, look over there, look at all those skid marks on the runway."

A voice from the seats in front pops up,

"That's nothing, you're worried? You should see the skid marks in my underpants!"

My friend was also observing the other passengers, looking out for any suspicious, serious Middle Eastern looking males amongst the excited holidaymakers on board. The years 1967 through 1972 were the golden years of hijacking. The PLO (Palestinian Liberation Organisation) were hardly going to hijack a budget airway plane out of Birmingham, but it all added to the excitement of the holiday. We would regularly see TV news coverage of planes that had been hijacked and flown to remote airports, somewhere in the Middle East. The passengers (hostages) would sit for days, inside the planes, strapped in their seats, with little food or water and no air conditioning, whilst the hijackers negotiated their demands with the authorities. Most hijackings during the sixties' decade, were, at first, associated with Cuba, and later, with the Middle East. Between the years 1961 and 1973, a total of 160 planes in American airspace, alone, were hijacked.

The longest hijacking incident to ever take place was during 1968, when PLO militants hijacked an El Al plane, starting at Rome and diverting it to Algiers. A number of hostages were held captive for forty days, only to be released after a boycott by international pilots. In 1970, Palestinian gunmen forced three planes, one from the UK, one from the USA and one from Switzerland, and forced them to land in Jordon. A number of hostages were held for twenty-four days whilst negotiations were ongoing, and finally freed in exchange for seven Palestinian prisoners.

My favourite hijacking story is the one that happened in November 1971, when one afternoon a nondescript man in Oregon USA, visited North Orient Airlines, and booked a one-way ticket to Seattle.

The middle-aged man was smartly dressed. On boarding the flight, he casually took his seat, and while waiting for the flight to take off, he ordered a whisky and soda. A short time later, whilst underway, he handed a stewardess a note, indicating that he was carrying a bomb in his hand luggage, and that she should sit with him. He opened his bag to give her a glimpse of the contents of wires and some red coloured sticks that resembled dynamite. He, then, dictated a message to her and instructed her to hand it to the captain of the plane. The message she handed to the captain demanded that when the plane arrived in Seattle, he be provided with four parachutes and US$200,000 in used notes. When the flight landed in Seattle, he released the flight's thirty-six passengers and some crewmembers, in exchange for the money and parachutes.

The plane took off again in the direction of Mexico, and somewhere between Seattle and the Mexican border, the man, who went by the name of Dan Cooper, parachuted out of the back of the plane and disappeared into the night. Cooper's fate remains one of the great unsolved mysteries to this day.

And so, we arrived in Majorca without incident, and found the Spanish experience to be a complete contrast to the great British holiday. Instead of imposing our culture on our hosts, this was a period of time that the British working class were beginning to appreciate and embrace the customs and lifestyles of our European neighbours. How we enjoyed seeing the sunshine every day, beautiful tanned girls around the hotel pool and at the beach parties, the bars open day and night, the boat trips and barbeques, the fiestas, the flamenco show, the vino, the sangria and the bull fights, *a symbol of Spanish culture,* which in later years, its popularity has decreased, and is now considered cruel and barbaric by most. How cool it was to learn and speak a few words in a foreign language, "Hey, *camarero*, two *cervezas* and one white *vino* por favor!"

For the first time in our lives, we would order a bottle of wine with a meal, we sampled garlic with our food, which for Brits was taboo, and typically smelly and foreign because it gave you bad breath. In the UK, it was considered lazy to sleep during the day time, but some of the lads would shamelessly disappear in the afternoon, saying they were going for a siesta, which sounds better than, "Going for a sleep," or, "Getting my head down," but was well-deserved after a late-night clubbing. There was the olive oil on every table, which we didn't know what to do with. There would normally be a small bottle of olive oil in the medicine cabinet back home, kept and used warm for earache, to lubricate squeaky door hinges or for baby's chapped skin.

Kissing on each cheek as a form of greeting was quite normal for the locals, where a nod of the head and a grunt was about all we did. This habit seems to have caught on back home, but it doesn't appear so natural to see the Brits do it, they look awkward and not so intimate.

We enjoyed the en suite hotel rooms and the habit of taking showers two or three times a day, and then there was that extra thing in the bathroom that we didn't know exactly what it was for, until it came up during a conversation in the bar one evening, when one of the lads mentioned that he had a thing next to his toilet with a sprinkler in it for washing his feet and swimming trunks, after the beach. And so, it went…

"It's not for that you dick-head, it's for washing your genitals after you have used the toilet."

"But there's no seat on it, and anyway, you would have to be careful if you turn the hot water on first, you would burn your balls."

"It's a French invention because they like lots of sex and use it before and after they do it."

"You guys don't know jack-shit, it's called a '*bidet*', which is a French word for pony. It got its name because when you use it, you have crouch over it the same way you sit on a horse. People need to practice how to use it."

"Hmm, nice if you can adjust the water pressures around your anus, I bet women enjoy using it!"

"Little kids could use it as a drinking fountain!"

The bidet would seem to be one custom that the British have not imported from our continental cousins, in spite of it being in use for over 300 years. It is believed that one of its functions was for the reasons of contraception.

The holiday in Spain, for me, was the last major event I shared with my close friends and workmates of that amazing decade. I went to sea working on many types of merchant ships, as a marine engineer, before emigrating to Brazil in 1979, where I found work in the oil and gas industry, and sometime later moving (with a family) to live and work in Dubai.

Chapter 16
Headlines, Iconic Moments

All I know is what I read in the papers, and that's an alibi for my ignorance.

W. Rogers.

I suppose there are no more, or less, iconic moments today, as there were during the sixties' decade. It's just that we are so well-informed these days, through the news media and social networks, that our interests are not stimulated, as they were at that time. Whilst growing up, I may have taken a slight interest in what was going on and making the news, but there were far more important things going on in my world. I was a young man, finding my way at work in the car factory, there were the fashions to worry about, the music scene, the football on Saturday, beer money, the weekend, and to impose my mod culture along with the crowd. So, what I mean to say is, I didn't really care about what was going on outside my world. However, on reflection, there were some interesting iconic moments during that decade which are worth re-visiting.

In 1960, an average house in the U.K. cost £2,550, the average weekly wage £15, sliced bread became available in the shops, the first episode of Coronation Street was screened, which was a supposedly a 16-part drama series, which has been running continuously until this day, The Beatles were formed and Penguin Books was cleared of obscenity for publishing '*Lady Chatterley's Lover*'.

Lady Chatterley's Lover was first secretly published in Italy, during 1928, but was banned in the United Kingdom until 1960, at which time, the publishers won an obscenity trial which had been lodged against them. The trial was a major public event, which put the obscenity law to the test, resulting in the book, written by D.H. Lawrence, becoming, possibly, the most notorious novel in British literature history. The book became renowned for its story of a sexual relationship and explicit descriptions of sex and the use of (at the time) unprintable four-letter words. The obvious reason, that once released, the first print of 200,000 copies, sold out immediately (London's largest bookshop, sold its 300 copies in fifteen minutes), with similar stories all over the country, and in a short time, it had sold over three million copies. The main case against the book was its use of four-letter words, as it used the words 'fuck' and 'cunt' frequently.

During the mid-sixties, grubby, well-thumbed copies of the book would turn up in the school playground or workplace and lent out for a couple of days to friends and workmates. I don't believe anybody of our calibre ever read the book from cover to cover or understood the supposedly literature merit the story contained, which reputedly helped the publisher win the obscenity case. I think, a couple of nights, sitting in bed, thumbing the pages for erotic parts, was all that was needed.

The story is around a young, married woman who marries a wealthy upper-class country gentleman and becomes 'Lady Chatterley'. Her husband, Sir Clifford Chatterley, returns from the Great War injured from the waist down, which results in a physical and emotional neglect of his wife that distances the couple. Lady Chatterley's frustration leads her into an affair with the estate's gamekeeper, whereby the story highlights differences between intellectuals and the working class, and that love can only happen with the element of body and not just the mind. Lady Chatterley's Lover went on to outsell the Holy Bible that year, which must have upset a number of church leaders, which I can imagine some saying under their breath, "That DH Lawrence is a fucking cunt!"

During 1962, a British band called The Tornadoes, had a number one hit in the USA with a song called, '*Telstar*'. They were the first British band to have a single reach number one in the US Hot 100, and Telstar was also number one in the UK singles chart. It was 10th July 1962 when Telstar 1 was launched and soared into space from Cape Canaveral Florida. And so, the world became a little smaller when the world's first active communications satellite became the first to send TV programmes, telephone calls (supplementing landlines) and images point to point, across the Atlantic. The phrase, 'live, via satellite', came first with Telstar, and those satellites that followed it into space, contributing to today's modern world. Telstar, a collaboration between US, French, and British broadcasting agencies, weighed only 171 pounds and was 34 inches in length. Originally, the Telstar satellites could only transmit events for twenty minutes at a time, as they orbited the Earth but laid the groundwork for the satellites of today, which hover at one point above the earth. Mobile phones, satellite TV and communications that we take for granted today, were science fiction and fragments of the imagination all those years ago. Telstar is apparently still orbiting Earth and during its short lifespan, handled over 400 phones, telegraph, and TV transmissions, but stopped functioning in November 1962, when the satellite failed, due to the effects of radiation.

Nelson Mandela was arrested on 5th August 1962, and later sentenced to life imprisonment for conspiracy against the state and plans to overthrow South Africa's apartheid rule, he went on to serve 27 years, 18 of which were hard labour, on the notorious Robben Island. He was only set free in 1990, after a long ongoing worldwide campaign to release him. I took an opportunity to visit Robben Island while I was in South Africa, sometime during the nineties. Robben Island twelve kilometres from Cape Town has a long history but is best known for its institutional brutality, imprisonment and its attempt to crush the moral of those who opposed apartheid – the most famous of these is Nelson Mandela.

I went out to the island aboard the ex-prison boat Suzen Kruker. My guide was an ex-political prisoner, who had spent eighteen years on the island, during the same time as Mandela. We talked at length, as he showed me around such places as the rock quarry, where political prisoners were made to work long hours during the hot summers and freezing winters, sometimes for no other reason than moving heavy rocks from one side of the quarry to the other. We visited the small prison cell where Nelson Mandela spent a large part of his life. There was little fresh water on the island and washing was generally in saltwater. He explained to me how he was arrested for attending an ANC (African National Congress banned from 1960 to 1990 by the white South African Government) meeting in Cape Town, charged and shipped out to the island. He described the mental torture inflicted by the prison authorities such as intercepting and withholding prisoners' mail or spreading false rumours of family and friends that were untrue. One visit from an immediate family member was allowed every six months, but most often cancelled without reason.

We visited the communal prison cell, where he spent his eighteen years, and he pointed out to me the small area on the floor where he slept amongst the other prisoners, and a white line behind which they had to stand to attention before first light for roll-call every morning.

During explanations, he would suddenly stop talking and go into a trance for a minute or two, as if his mind was drifting back to those prisoner days, then he would come out of it and just carry on the conversation where he left off.

The toilets, he explained, were where the young prisoners took lessons, during the night, on how to read and write using candles, paper and pencils smuggled to them by the criminal prisoners, who were also serving on the island and did meaningless jobs around the prison buildings.

The most amazing thing about this man was that, after all he had been through, he did not show any animosity or speak aggressively of the persons responsible for taking away eighteen years of his life. Nelson Mandela went on to be South Africa's first black president.

For thirteen days during October 1962, the world held its breath, when the United States and the Soviet Union became engaged in a standoff, after an American spy plane had photographed Soviet nuclear-armed ballistic missiles being assembled on Cuban soil, whilst on a reconnaissance mission over Cuba.

After the 1959 Cuban, leftist revolution, whereby Fidel Castro and his revolutionaries seized control of the country, and the USA had severed diplomatic and economic ties with Cuba, Castro's Communist Party aligned themselves with the Soviet Union. It was during the time when the USA and the Soviet Union were engaged in the Cold War. The US had attempted to overthrow Castro's government earlier during April 1961, when the CIA financed and trained a group of 1,500 exiled Cuban refugees, made up of landowners, landlords and businessmen, that ended in total failure. The invasion landing point was the '*Bay of Pigs*', an open swampy area in the south of the island, with no place for the invading army to take refuge if discovered. Hours before the invasion, the CIA flew a bomber from Nicaragua painted, to look like a Cuban plane, to bomb Cuban military sites, but it missed most of its targets. During the invasion, as many as 1,200 members of the exiled brigade, surrendered and were imprisoned, and more than 100 killed by the Cuban forces. A number managed to escape by sea. In 1962, more than 1,000 men taken prisoner at the 'Bay of Pigs' invasion were returned to the USA, in exchange for a ransom of US$ 53 million in food and medical supplies, donated by US companies and businesses.

On 22nd October 1962, President Kennedy addressed the nation on a TV news broadcast, notifying the American people of the presence of the soviet ballistic missiles, just ninety miles from US shores. He went on to explain his decision to place a naval blockade around Cuba, and that he was prepared to use military force to neutralise the threat to the nation's security, if necessary. The world feared it was on the brink of nuclear war.

The situation was eventually resolved, and disaster avoided, after negotiations between the Americans and the Soviet leader, Nikita Khrushchev. Khrushchev agreed to remove his missiles from Cuba, in exchange for the US promising not to invade Cuba and removing missiles the Americans had placed some years earlier in Turkey. Kennedy agreed, and secretly removed the US missiles from Turkey, without the knowledge of the public.

Che Guevara, the Argentinian revolutionist, aided Castro in overthrowing the Cuban government, and became his second in command, and later held several political positions in Castro's newly-formed government. Sometime after the failed Bay of Pigs invasion, Guevara sent a letter to President Kennedy, thanking him and saying that before the invasion, the revolution was weak, but now it was stronger than ever. Sometime during 1965, Guevara left Cuba and went on to support other guerrilla activities elsewhere around the world.

Che Guevara, to this day, is remembered as a legendary icon of the sixties. His name is associated with rebellion, revolution and socialism, and even today, his life continues to be a subject of great public interest, especially with the younger generation. His face, taken from a 1960 photograph titled '*Guerrillero Heroico*', is portrayed around the world, on the cover of magazines, t-shirts, caps, key rings, posters and people proudly portray it as a symbol of the underdog, the idealist, the martyr, and with each generation, Guevara's life continues to be explored and defined.

What his admirers don't want to hear however, that there are many Cuban nationals that witnessed Guevara's cruelty in assassinating many innocent Cubans, or those that dared to oppose or disagree with himself or Castro. When he was a member of Castro's government, he is said to have ordered the execution of large numbers of political prisoners without trial. Over the years, propaganda, painting Guevara as a Robin Hood type of character, that chose the life of a militant to help the poor of the world, when in fact, he was simply pursuing an ego, has been a very lucrative business for many.

Che Guevara was executed in Bolivia by government troops on 9th October 1967, at the age of 39, having gone there and formed a liberation army, in an attempt to bring down the Bolivian government. His hands were cut off for proof and fingerprint identification and the body hidden. In 1995, a search uncovered Guevara's remains at the town of Vallegrande and sent to Cuba, where they were laid to rest.

Castro died of natural causes on 25th November 2016, at the ripe old age of ninety. It is reputed that there were hundreds of attempts to assassinate him during his lifetime, including bizarre attempts or ideas, planned by the CIA, which included, the exploding cigar. A box of his favourite cigars was laced with botulinum toxin, strong enough to kill anyone who put one in their mouth. The contaminated diving suit with a fungus that would produce a chronic skin disease, and a large painted seashell that would explode if disturbed. Castro was an avid fan of scuba diving. A poisoned pen with a needle so fine the victim would not notice the insertion. Recruiting Castro's lover to poison him with pills dropped in his drink that would kill him in seconds. She didn't do it. When they came together, they made love instead.

Politicians and politics meant little to me, although I was always a somewhat fascinated with Harold Wilson. He would appear being interviewed with his wife Mary by his side, with an appearance like any sixties' working-class married couple. He had a strange (which I know now), Yorkshire accent and when being interviewed, would stand with one hand in his pocket and a pipe raised in the other hand. Harold Wilson was a Labour MP, who won two elections, serving twice as Britain's Prime Minister, from 1964 to 1970 and again from 1974 to 1976.

Even I remember Wilson's legendry devaluation speech, that went on air in November 1967, to explain to the nation that the pound (sterling) was to be devalued by 14% and the situation of the country's trade balance etc. He went on to say, "*It does not mean that the pound here in Britain, in your pocket or purse or in your bank has been devalued.*" '*The pound in your pocket*' went on to become a sixties' catchphrase. It was Wilson who first made the statement we still hear today, "*A week is a long time in politics*."

Many courageous legislations were implemented under the Wilson government; they ended capital punishment, legalised abortion, decriminalised homosexuality, promoted women in politics, introduced the race relations act and equal pay act and went on to build homes at the rate of 400,000 a year.

Wilson was unpopular in Europe, and against joining the then-European Union, he wanted to keep the commonwealth united. A thing we should give Harold Wilson credit for, is his diplomacy with the USA; he was not stupid and should be remembered for keeping British troops out of the Vietnam War, despite repeated American requests. It is reputed that Harold Wilson was Queen Elizabeth's favourite prime minister.

During March 1966, John Lennon, in an interview with a journalist from the London Evening Standard, made a comment, which almost destroyed The Beatles reputation in America. Just a couple of days before The Beatles were to start a major US tour, and five months after the interview first appeared, an American magazine picked up on his comments and published it as a headline story, with little resemblance to the original text. A sudden outburst of protests broke out across the USA. During the interview in London, Lennon made the following statement: "*Christianity will go. It will vanish and shrink. I needn't argue with that; I'm right and I will be proved right. We're more popular than Jesus is now; I don't know which will go first, rock 'n' roll or Christianity. Jesus was all right, but his disciples were thick and ordinary. It's them twisting it that ruins it for me.*"

The Jesus controversy was the perfect opportunity for Christian groups, religious radio stations and DJs who were opposed to the rock scene, the British invasion and The Beatles tremendous popularity, to get the publicity and media coverage they yearned for themselves. American radio stations began banning The Beatles music, and religious groups demonstrated with banners, '*John Lennon is Satan*', '*God loves you, do The Beatles?*', and so on! Fans were encouraged to boycott the band and burn their Beatles records, magazines and souvenirs.

Brian Epstein, The Beatles' manager, fearing for the safety of the band members, offered to pay a million dollars to cancel the tour. Maureen Cleave, who conducted the interview in London, came forward to clarify the comments made in her interview, and said, "John was certainly not comparing The Beatles to Christ. He was simply observing that, so weak was the state of Christianity, The Beatles were, to many people, better known."

In spite of the hostility, threats and controversy, the tour went ahead as planned. Upon arriving in America, the band conducted a press conference as soon as they stepped off the plane to address the incident. Lennon, confidently, opened his address, by saying, "*If I'd said, Television is more popular than Jesus, I might have got away with it!*", and concluded his statement by reminding promoters that it is well within their rights to cancel their planned appearances.

The demonstrations continued throughout the tour, and eventually John was encouraged to make an official apology. In front of thirty journalists in a hotel suite, he said, "I'm not anti-God, anti-Christ or anti-religion. I was not knocking it. I was not saying we're better or greater, or comparing us with Jesus Christ as a person or God as a thing or whatever it is. I happened to be talking to a friend, and I used the word Beatles as a remote thing, Beatles like other people see us. I said they are having more influence on kids and things than anything else, including Jesus. I said it in that way, which was the wrong way. I apologise if that will make you happy. I still don't know quite what I've done. I've tried to tell you what I did do, but if you want me to apologise, if that will make you happy, then – Okay, I'm sorry."

The tour, consisting of nineteen performances, seventeen shows in the US and two in Canada, was the last commercial concert tour that The Beatles performed.

On 20th April 1968, at a Conservative Association meeting in Birmingham, the MP for Wolverhampton, Enoch Powell, delivered a speech that criticised the rates of immigration entering the UK, which split the nation in two. For many, mainly the white working-class, he became a hero, equally, the policy-making establishment despised him, denouncing him as a racist.

To comprehend the gist of Enoch Powell's, (which became known as) the '*Rivers of Blood*' speech, the following is a very short excerpt:

Quote. *It almost passes belief that at this moment 20 or 30 additional immigrant children are arriving from overseas in Wolverhampton alone every week, and that means 15 or 20 additional families, a decade or two hence. Those whom the gods wish to destroy, they first make mad. We must be mad, literally mad, as a nation to be permitting the annual inflow of some 50,000 dependents, who are, for the most part, the material of the future growth of the immigrant-descended population. It is like watching a nation busily engaged in heaping up its own funeral pyre. So insane are we that we actually permit unmarried persons to immigrate for the purpose of founding a family with spouses and fiancés, whom they have never seen.* Unquote

Several polls taken after the speech showed that between 67% and 82% of the population agreed with Powell's opinions, even so, his own party criticised him, saying the speech was a blatant demonstration of racism, although it was later claimed that the large public following Powell, attracted with his views on immigration, helped the conservatives to win the 1970 general election.

During January 1969, Powell appeared on, and was interviewed by David Frost, on his evening television news show. During the interview Frost asked him whether or not he was a racialist. Powell replied,

Quote: *It depends on how you define the word 'racialist'. If you mean being conscious of the differences between men and nations, and from that, races, then we are all racialists. However, if you mean a man who despises a human being because he belongs to another race, or a man who believes that one race is inherently superior to another, then the answer is emphatically 'no'*. Unquote.

To this day, Powell's name comes up during debates and the subject of immigration, continue to divide the nation.

During March 1967, a Liberian registered oil tanker, SS Torrey Canyon, ran aground on the Seven Stones Reef off the south-west coast of England, spilling an estimated 36 million gallons (100,000 tons) of crude oil into the sea. The ship was on its way from Kuwait to the Milford Haven oil refinery, in Wales. It was the first globally televised environmental disaster and served as a wakeup call to the potential of future disasters of such a scale. Beaches as far away as Guernsey and Brittany in France were left knee-deep in black sludge, and thousands of marine mammals and sea birds were killed. More than two million gallons of chemicals were sprayed over the affected areas, which went on to create as much damage as the oil spill itself. The plan was for the chemicals to break down the oil slicks and allow it to disperse by natural bacteria. But instead, it killed all the marine life it came into contact with and so, only contributed to the disaster.

Following unsuccessful attempts to pull the ship from the reef, there was an effort to burn off the oil spilling from the distressed vessel, by setting it on fire, in way of air strikes by the Royal Airforce. In total, 161 bombs. 16 rockets, 1,500 tons of napalm and 44,500 litres of kerosene were used. The ship sank, but the fires were extinguished by the heavy seas. It was described as a spectacle not seen since the war, but not a particularly good day's work for the pilots, as only 23 of the 41 bombs actually hit the huge target. The Torrey Canyon was a first-generation type super tanker. The oil on board belonged to BP (British Petroleum), who ironically were selling the detergent in enormous quantities that was being used to try and disperse the spill.

Invaluable lessons were learned from the UK's biggest ever oil spill, ranging from protection of the environment, response methods and materials to revised rules and regulations to shipping. The inquiry, following, the incident found the Italian captain was to blame because of taking a shortcut to the oil terminal to save time. Additionally, a design fault was found in the steering system, where, if the autopilot was accidently left switched on, the helmsman was unable to override and steer the vessel.

Although the Torrey Canyon was the first major disaster of its kind, it would not be the last.

20th September 1967, the passenger liner SS Queen Elizabeth 2 (QE2), belonging to the Cunard Steamship Company was launched. Built by John Brown Company and Clyde Bank Shipbuilders, she was designed for the transatlantic service, from her home port of Southampton UK to New York.

The QE2 set off on her maiden voyage on 2nd May 1969, crossing the Atlantic in four days, 16 hours and 35 minutes, making her the fastest passenger ship in service for 39 years from her launch, until being retired in 2008. The QE 2 stood for everything that was great about Britain at that time, a marvel of engineering, a unique design and razor-sharp bow, that allowed her to cut through the Atlantic at 34 knots, when the average speed of others was 10 to 12 knots. During that time, the Cunard liner completed 1,400 voyages, over six million nautical miles while carrying 2.5 million passengers and went on to complete over 25 world tours.

The QE2 was the last oil-fired passenger steamship to run a scheduled liner service, until being refitted with diesel electric propulsion during 1986/87.

Following an intensive refurbishment, the QE2 re-opened in April 2018, and started a new life as a floating hotel, restaurant and entertainment centre, laying afloat at Port Rashid Dubai, with her previous port of registration on the stern replaced with 'Dubai'.

The Time Magazine, on October 25th, 1968, wrote that 'Faster Higher Stronger' is the motto of the Olympic Games, '*Angrier, Nastier and Uglier*' better describes the scene in Mexico City last week.

There had been growing social unrest and protests in Mexico, months before the 1968 Olympics were due to take place there. Initially, the protesters were protesting for greater civil and democratic rights, against political and social suppression, however, as the Olympics drew near, the protesters began to show contempt for the games with such slogans as, '*We don't want Olympics, we want revolution*'.

Ten days before the start of the Summer Olympic Games, a peaceful gathering of protesters in one of Mexico City's main public squares was broken up, when the Mexican government sent in some 5,000 soldiers and 200 armoured cars to disperse the crowds. Hundreds of civilians were killed when the soldiers opened fire and drove into the protesters. Over a thousand were arrested. The games went ahead, in spite of the concern of competing countries.

The games were taking place during the height of racial tensions worldwide. Dr Martin Luther King had been assassinated a few months earlier, the Black Power Movement was gaining momentum, and groups of black athletes were contesting the invitations to Rhodesia and South Africa to participate, due to these countries practice of apartheid. A group of US athletes, which called themselves the Olympic Project for Human Rights, decided that the games would be an opportunity to protest for better treatment of black athletes and black people around the world and competed hoping to increment change.

The iconic image of the 1968 Olympic Games was the 200-meter, race when two American athletes, gold medallist Tommie Smith and bronze medallist John Carlos, took their places on the podium to receive their medals, wearing black socks no shoes and civil rights badges. They faced the flag and when the national anthem played, lowered their heads and each raised a fist with a black glove, in solidarity with the Black Freedom Movement. The two athletes were subsequently expelled from the games, following a threat that the whole US team would be banned from the Olympic Village if they didn't leave.

The third man on the podium, was, white Australian silver medallist Peter Norman. He didn't raise his fist, but also wore an Olympic Project for Human Rights badge. It is said that it was him that encouraged Smith and Carlos to wear the black gloves. Norman felt strongly about human rights in his own country, relating to the treatment and suppression of the Australian indigenous Aborigine people. In spite of him making qualifying time to participate, he was not allowed to represent Australia in the 1972 games and played no part in the Australian games hosted in 2000. Both Smith and Carlos were pallbearers at Norman's funeral after he died of a heart attack in 2006.

Another moment to remember in the 1968 games, was the 400-meter hurdles. Britain's David Hemery made the final, beat the reigning champion Geoff Vander stock and shattered the world record. BBC's commentator was in hysterics, as they reached the finishing line announcing the first and second before, coming up with one of those iconic moments in sport when he screamed, *"And who care's who's third – it doesn't matter."*

Well it did matter. Britain's second-ranked hurdler, John Sherwood climbed on the podium to receive the bronze medal.

On January 30th, 1969, The Beatles played their farewell concert on the rooftop of their recording studio, Apple Corps, in London. They previewed songs for a forthcoming album, '*Let It Be*', but the impromptu set was intercepted by the Metropolitan Police after 42 minutes.

On 4th March 1969, the Kray twins, Ronald and Reginald, were found guilty for the murder of Jack McVitie, alias Jack the Hat. The court was told how Jack 'The Hat' McVitie was repeatedly stabbed by Reginald Kray, in a north London flat. while his brother held him down. Their elder brother, Charles, was convicted to helping to dispose of the body. The court were also told of an earlier accusation of how Ronald Kray shot dead George Cornell in front of customers at the Blind Beggar pub in 1966, for calling him a 'fat poof' (poof or puff being a slang word for gay during that time). The Kray twins were both sentenced to life imprisonment, with a recommendation they should be detained for a minimum of 30 years, the longest sentences ever passed at the Old Bailey for murder. Charles Kray was jailed for 10 years

People spend their honeymoon in different ways. John Lennon, who married Yoko Ono on 20th March 1969, spent theirs in bed in the presidential suite at the Amsterdam Hotel for a week, inviting the world's media into their hotel room each day, from 9 a.m. to 9 p.m. The Vietnam War was at its peak at this time, and they wanted to encourage the use of non-violent protests against wars and explore new ideas to promote peace. The press didn't know what to expect but arrived to find the couple sitting in bed, wearing pyjamas just wanting to talk about peace. Two signs over the bed read, '*Hair Peace*' and '*Bed Peace'*.

A week later, they went to Vienna to hold a conference on '*Bagism*', something John wanted to promote. John and Yoko appeared, both together, sitting in an enormous canvas bag. According to John and Yoko, a person could not be judged by others, if enclosed in a bag, on the basis of their race, age, colour of skin, length of hair, attire etc. The concept of *Bagism* is interactivity amongst people without prejudice.

I am not sure I could buy that! If I went to meet someone and found them sitting in a bag, I would judge them right away, "What the fuck are they trying to hide from me?"

A second '*bed-in*' happened at the Queen Elizabeth Hotel in Montreal Canada on May 26th. They had intended to hold it in New York, but at the time, Lennon, was not allowed into the US because of a cannabis conviction from the previous year. For seven days, they conducted interviews and discussions with the press, covered by the Canadian Broadcasting Corporation, and transmitted all over the world. It was here, in the hotel room, that on 1st June, together with celebrity and counterculture friends, they recorded the notorious peace anthem, '*Give Peace a Chance*'.

In the December of 1969, John and Yoko posted billboards in eleven major cities worldwide, with the message, "War is Over, If You Want it – Happy Christmas from John and Yoko."

Lennon recorded a number of songs dedicated to world peace. The two most successful, but most simple and beautiful have to be, '*Imagine*' and, '*Happy Christmas, (War is Over)*'. But sadly, it's not.

During the sixties, great advances were made in the research of fibre optics, as a practical use in communications. During 1965, two British research scientists, Charles Kao and George Hockman, working with Standard Telephones and

Cables, discovered that attenuation of fibre optic cables could be used as a means to carry electronic information.

By the early 1990s, and with the coming of the computer age, fibre optic cables started to be laid all across the world, and today fibre communications are present in almost every country and the main principle of the modern communications infrastructure.

In the 1964, James Bond movie, '*Goldfinger*', secret agent 007 was almost sliced in two by a laser beam. It did not look good for him, even though back then we had no idea what a laser beam was. One has to wonder, what life would be like today, without fibre optic cables and laser beams, even though very few people have any conception on how they work. The first practical laser was developed back in 1960, and over time the use of this tool has increased and can now be applied to a wide range of technologies. Today, in the home, we have lasers in our CD and DVD players that read the sound, just as the needle did on our vinyl records. In the office, we have laser printers and it's a laser that reads the barcode on the packages, and price tags when we shop. The inscriptions on tombstones, made of granite or limestone are carved out with large powerful lasers, and jewellers can inscribe minute identification numbers on diamonds for their files. In the medical industry, lasers are used in many types of surgery because they are more precise and hygienic than surgical instruments; they are also used for eye, and dental surgery, and can be used for removing tumours.

And, thank goodness, they can also be used to remove tattoos, which must be useful with the current phase from people of all types getting tattooed. I find it most aggravating when I am travelling, and some naïve guy gets on the plane, dressed in a gym shirt and shorts, just so everyone can see the tattoos on his flabby white arms and legs. For me, a person has to earn his tattoos, like the deckhand or boson of a ship, an ex-convict, a gang member or mixed martial arts free fighter. How ridiculous does an accountant or a shop assistant look with a snake dragon or tiger, and Chinese inscriptions tattooed over him? But for sure, lasers have become indispensable to most people's daily lives!

Advances in medicine included the first human heart transplant, which was in carried out by Doctor Christian Barnard in Cape Town, South Africa, during December 1967. The patient only lived for eighteen days, succumbing in the end to pneumonia. microwave ovens and ATMs (Automatic Teller Machines) were introduced during the sixties, also pull tabs on canned drinks, silicone breast implants and dairy cows were not happy when non-dairy creamer appeared in the shops.

Chapter 17
Back to the Future

Life can only be understood backwards, but it must be lived forwards.

Soren Kierkegaard.

And so, I finish my memories, the way I started. Sitting at a bar in Bangkok. One of my favourite places here, is a small nondescript bar, hidden away towards the end of Silom Road's notorious Soi 4. The bar, '*4 Sports*', is owned by a taciturn, very pleasant English man, who manages and imbibes simultaneously, with calm ease, and his ebullient Thai wife. Apparently, the owner, an avid Norwich City supporter, opened the bar some years ago, with the intention of attracting a clientele who followed sports, especially football. Hence the name 4 Sports. But as you will see below, he got more than he bargained for! It's an ideal place to meet and get to know expats, local Thais and tourists. My drinking buddies here are varied, some, typical of those Bangkok secretive vagrant types I described at the beginning of the story, others, ex-executives that are no longer active, retired from high profile jobs, who have chosen to pass their twilight days in Bangkok, or make it their home, for reasons of their own. Informal bars and meeting places such as 4 Sports, are not on the tourist map, and are only found in the shadows of the entertainment areas or by ferreting and exploring the back streets of the city.

In an earlier chapter, I was writing about growing up in Coventry during the sixties' decade. How much this bar and its different characters remind me of those days, when, as a young man, I drank and chatted freely, with my friends and workmates in the pubs and the working men's clubs?

Here, the regulars, and a few visitors, tend to congregate around the dimly lit half round counter on bar stools, at the far end of the bar; tourists prefer sitting at the front of the bar, observing what's going on outside, along the rumbustious Soi 4 (street). Here, our evenings normally start courteously, discussing amongst ourselves; the day's events, local news or the sports being televised on a plasma TV on the wall. But, for various reasons, and as the alcohol intake levels increase, the evenings do not always end in such a relaxed manner!

It is difficult to describe the diversity of my drinking colleagues in this bar, or those expats of various nationalities, that come and go, or those that always come to visit whenever they are in Bangkok. Their backgrounds couldn't be more different. Some examples would be, the unkempt Irish guy I can only describe as a likable rogue, who walks the streets of Bangkok by night, associates with the shady characters in those places where you can only find liquor, after the bars have closed, and then sleeps during the day. If he doesn't appear in the bar for a week, we fear the worst, 'locked up or deported', but he always bounces back! An elderly US diplomat, who has served in eight countries worldwide, that sits at the bar in his baseball cap, chewing gum, smoking a 'Kaywoodie Pipe', and goes apeshit at the mention of Donald Trump (there are no grey areas with American diplomats, only black and white!) An English restaurant owner, who has his own stool at the corner of the bar. A good listener, and probably the least opinionated of the bunch. A loveable, retired Irishman, with that wonderful Irish humour, intelligent and well-read, who was born and brought up in a small village in Ireland, where the eldest son in the family is normally groomed to become a catholic priest. However, in his own words, he says, that one day, whilst he was growing up, he came to realise, that, not only was he an atheist, he was also gay! A short, very stocky, heavy Australian guy, who captained his own fishing boat off the coast of Queensland. He will listen to a debate at the bar flow quietly until he feels it merits his opinion. He then gives it all he's got, in true Aussie fashion, like someone had wound him up and let him go. The air goes blue with four letter words, in a gravelly broad Australian accent, until he has had his say and goes back to quietly drinking his beer. He has been known to drink until he falls off the stool. God knows how they find the man-power to lift him back up again. A much travelled, ex-Canadian government official and UN administrator, who cleverly manipulates or controls the climate of the disputes and disagreements as they develop. We do disagree, often! A budding, Danish, Bitcoin investor who appears to have disappeared from the scene, just as the Bitcoin did, but he will be back. These are just a few examples. As I mentioned earlier, one never really knows who we are sitting next to, at the bar in Bangkok. One of those odd reasons we love it here.

The degree and diversity of conversations never cease to amaze me. As the drinks flow, the topics deviate from sports, movies, travel, politics, world affairs, you name it. Probably the only thing we all agree on, is that the interaction in this small bar is unique in today's world of political correctness, and where expressionless people everywhere seem to prefer to sitting, looking at their mobile phones and gadgets.

And so, I sit back in amazement at the conversations. Who's going to win the French Tennis open? Why should Ronaldo be considered the best football player in the world and not Messi? Who will benefit from China's controversial new Silk Road? What's the future of the European Union? Why is it when crazy people hear voices in their head, they are being told to kill people, why don't they tell them to wash the car or help with the housework? Who played James Bond in '*Her Majesty's Service*'? What was Alfred Hitchcock terrified of? The debates can get rowdy, and go on until the early hours, a rare opportunity to be able to express ourselves in such a way in today's senseless world, and what is more intriguing is the wealth of general knowledge between a small group of people.

Of course, the more alcohol we drink the more knowledgeable we become, until some clever dick throws something in to test our ignorance such as, “In the study of anatomy, of the psyche and psychotherapy, and how ancestral archetypes live in us, how would you compare the Jung Psychology Theories with those of Sigmund Freud?”

One of my favourites was, when a conversation at the bar, erupted as to how Britain got involved in World War 1. The Canadian gentleman, without missing a beat and with a pint of beer in one hand, went on to give an amazing detailed explanation, of the sequence of events, which left his drinking buddies, for a moment, with overwhelming admiration. I will not attempt to match his knowledge or details of the events with names, places, dates etc. but it was something like the following,

First, he explained that there had been a number of events leading up to the unrest in and around Europe before Britain entered the war. There was the Moroccan Crisis 1905-1906, provoked by the Germans to cause tensions between France and Britain, the Balkan Wars and the Bosnian Annexation Crisis, the Italian-Turkish War, and so on.

He went on to say that it was an incident where Archduke Franz Ferdinand of Austria and his wife were assassinated during a visit to the Bosnian capital Sarajevo, during June 1914 that triggered the course of events that followed. It was the excuse Austria and Hungry needed to declare war on its Balkan neighbour to eliminate the ‘Serbian threat’, and later invade Serbia, and so Austria commenced to bombard Belgrade, the Serbian capital.

In the meantime, Russia began partial troop mobilisation as a precaution of escalating unrest in the area. The Germans warned Russia about intervention and began to mobilise for war themselves.

Germany, then declared war on Russia. France and Belgium began full mobilisation.

Next, Germany declares war on France and invades neutral Belgium. Britain delivers an ultimatum to Germany, demanding withdrawal from Belgium. Germany ignores it.

Britain, some years earlier, had already entered into an alliance with France because of the threat from the German

Empire. France were already in an alliance with Russia, and the three became the core of the allied countries.

And so, Britain declares war on Germany, which draws in the British Empire, including Canada, Australia, New Zealand, India and South Africa into the war. If that's not enough, Austria and Hungary go on to declare war on Russia.

Some days later, I mentioned to him how interesting I thought his take on World War 1, was, but had to remind him about his explanation of events. He just shrugged, and said, "Me? I don't remember, anyway I know jack shit about WW1."

I believe, given the opportunity, myself and my colleagues from 4 Sports, could resolve most of the world's problems over a few glasses of beer. It's a bar where, on any given evening, there could be five or six different nationalities at the counter, people ranging from atheist to religious believers, in the middle of one of the seediest red-light districts of the city, and yet all get along, conflicts are resolved and different views taken into account. You never know who is going to walk through the door and be welcomed to the table. All people's views are welcomed and incorporated into the discussion

One thing that I have discovered since retiring and waking up from a lifetime of work, is that I now live in a completely different world to the one I thought I lived in! Social media is now at everyone's fingertips, and so-called experts in anything and everything, telling us how we should live our lives, is only leading to confusion and uncertainty.

I recently visited a bookstore, looking for something interesting to read and was amazed to see the number of self-help and well-being books on how to elevate and transform our lives that are on display. There was a shelf each, for fiction, non-fiction, memoirs, and travel, but two shelves for self-help and wellbeing. The books have inspiring titles, '*A Guide to Personal Empowerment*', '*Seven Ways to Resilience*', '*A Year of Positive Thinking*', but the one that did catch my attention and one that I would certainly endorse is, '*The Subtle Art of Not Giving a F*ck*'. How can we learn about life from a book? We have to live it! People who read these books need to take what they have learned, and apply it to how they live their lives, which I am not sure they understand. The wellness industry today is turning into a major business, just as the pharmaceutical is. Psychiatrists and life coaches are cashing in big time! Anyway, I settled for a book called the '*The Last Executioner*', the memoirs of Bangkok's notorious Bang Kwang prison executioner, who was responsible for executing fifty-five prisoners during his time in the prison service. The story, of his life as a young boy, becoming a member of a rock band, joining the prison service, and his descriptions of some cases, leading to the prisoners he executed, together with life in Bang Kwang Prison, probably teaches us more about life, than most of the self-help books on display. Read about people that have no hope, that live in a place with no hope, and then see how bad you feel!

When I glance around at people today in the street, shopping malls and trains, and compare them to those I grew up with during the sixties, I see a generation with faces that appear mentally and emotionally drained. People waste endless hours on social media, absorbing useless knowledge and trying to live out other people's fantasies, whilst neglecting and becoming out of balance to achieve their own. The key to life, in my generation, was not trying to learn what you didn't need to know, but follow what you wanted to do or be, then implementing what you learned and create your own, better world.

The opportunity to travel is said to be an education and an adventure, but with the information available today, people just don't experience the excitement of interfacing with strangers or getting lost when trying to find their way to some location or tourist attraction. They just stroll along, following the direction on Google maps in their phone, oblivious of all the interesting things going on and people around them. Their best friend, the phone, even translates for them when they are ordering food in the restaurant. Oh, and they only go to those places recommended on Trip Advisor. How much fun is that, visiting places that everyone knows about?

When I stepped off the plane in Sao Paulo, forty years ago, I did not speak the language, 'Portuguese', I had no contacts in that city of sixteen million people, and for sure didn't know my way around. All I had was the address of an employment agency that promised to find me a job. I got into a daily routine, which began with checking to see if the agency had any work lined up for me, which they didn't. I would then drift downtown. Over the next few weeks, I walked, bussed or took the metro and explored the whole city. I rubbed shoulders with Brazilians from all walks of life, from hookers in Bras, the notorious sleazy area where I stayed, businessmen in the city to families and relatives of friends I made. The city streets and squares were always lively, and full of hustle and bustle from people on the move. Street entertainers from all parts of South America entertained in the squares and on the street corners, clown-type characters, fire eaters, musicians. I got lost, I ate food I didn't like, I met friendly people and some not so friendly. There was never a dull moment, like a crowd chasing a pickpocket, who would run into the road and weave his way through a six lane traffic jam, taunting them by holding the wallet he had just stolen in the air with a 'come and get me' gesture, or the police dragging away a shoplifter who was resisting and screaming their innocence. What a contrast to Coventry, and what an adventure learning about another culture!

The downside was when I was tipped off by a German friend, explaining that the employment agency really had no intention of finding me a job. In fact, the longer I stayed out of work, the longer they could claim and pocket expenses that were being fabricated on my behalf daily. And so, as much as I was enjoying the life in Sao Paulo, my funds were becoming short and I needed to find work, so I packed up and took a bus the 429 kilometres to Rio de Janeiro. I grew up during the sixties. I was confident, adventurous, rebellious, and wanted to explore and meet people. What better place than Rio to do that? The best advice I ever had was from my mother.

Whenever I was going anywhere, she would always say, just as I was leaving home, *"If you can't be good then be careful,"* which I remember to this day, especially when I am planning doing something that I should not be doing. I remained in Brazil for eleven years.

It seems in today's world, there are a bunch of imprudent people that are determined to be offended by something or other, and have nothing better to do with their time. They voice their displeasure about trivial things on social media. How often do we read or hear people say, they were offended about something, often resulting with unjustified consequences, especially where race or gender is concerned? Who really cares if someone is offended or not? We all get offended all the time. How would they have survived in a factory, during the sixties or on a merchant ship thousands of miles from home, when a big red headed Scottish chief engineer knocks on your cabin door, after you have finished your watch in a stinking hot engine room, and doesn't ask, just says in a nice way, "Get your fucking ass on the deck and help the guys repair the windless." You could, of course, complain to the captain and tell him you were offended. On the flight from Dubai to Bangkok recently, the guy sitting next to me, with neither shoes nor socks, sat back in his seat and put his dirty feet up against the back of the seat, in front of him. I waited till I couldn't stand it any longer and told him to put his feet down. He gave me a strange look saying, "What's the problem?" I said, that the problem is, people have to eat from the tray that folds down from the back of the seat. He was 'offended', but I was 'offended' too! He was of a different culture, so I had to be careful, as in today's world he could have accused me of being racist.

Today's generation spend their time, adding new friends to Facebook, but in reality, many have no close friends at all. Instead of getting out there and fighting for social causes and getting involved in what they believe, many just post their grievances on the web, which may satisfy themselves, but makes no tangible difference to their cause at all. We have a problem whereby a small part of society is aggressively imposing their views on the majority. 'Real TV' television shows where ordinary people or celebrities are judged and ridiculed publicly, have taken the place of those non-fictional, informative programmes of the past that would make us think and test our intelligence. Movies full of violence, obnoxious plots and scripts with little plausibility have become the norm, whereby bold adventurous cinema has declined. In my mind, movie stars and celebrities are not important at all. Yes, they can be very talented and wonderful at what they do. But for me, the surgeon that operates and saves lives daily, the aircraft technicians that service the engines on the plane you are flying on, are far more important, and those people that dedicate their lives protecting the environment, saving animals from extinction or helping people less fortunate should be our heroes. *During the publication of this book, the COVID-19 virus occurred. The dedication, heroism and commitment of health workers all over the world, some sacrificing their own lives, I believe supports my case.* Movie stars are hypocrites, they don't think twice about taking a role in a movie that incites drugs, sex, violence and exploitation of the sexes, if there is enough money in it for themselves.

Kids today are becoming obese by sitting in the house all day. When they go outside, they cannot walk past a Baskin Robins, Pizza Hut, or Dunkin Donuts, without filling their face or walk through the shopping mall without a wrap in one hand and a smoothie in the other! It's sad to not see as many kids outside in the open spaces, using their imaginations anymore, and sad how technology has affected their lives. Those days as a carefree, young kid growing up, were some of the best days of my life.

Not a day goes by when I don't feel thankful that I grew up and went to work as a young man during the amazing sixties' decade, and the platform it gave me to appreciate everything and the challenges that were thrown at me later in life.

Having got that off my chest, I will finish my story.

Oh, the grumpy old expat mod in Bangkok!

Sitting alone in a bar the other day, deep in thought, looking into my beer glass, a fresh-faced young tourist guy came in and sat next to me. After some minutes he tried to start a conversation.

"Hi, are you living in Bangkok?"

"Naa."

"Just working here?"

"Naa."

"Tourist?"

"Naa."

"Just passing through, then?"

"Not exactly."

Silence for a few minutes, then…

"So, where you from exactly?"

After some thought I replied…

"I can't really say, I live on airplanes, trains and buses and hang out in different countries!"

I drank up, wished him a good day and left him with his thoughts.

Epilogue

So, what does one do to fill the time when retirement comes? Sitting, drinking in bars, or in front of the TV all day is not the answer. I decided that, teaching English to foreigners could be the way forward, so I took the TEFL (teach English as a foreign language) course whilst I was in Bangkok. I was the only native English speaker, amongst a group that included a Mexican, an Indian, an Iranian and French. I excelled, of course, over the first couple of weeks in the roll play, answering questions, conversation and pronunciation, until that is, the day the instructor looked at me and said, "Give me an example of a preposition?" I had no idea. To my embarrassment, the clever-ass Indian guy stands up, and says, "It's a word that links nouns and pronouns and other words in a sentence together."

The instructor looked at me again, and asked, "Then, what is an adverb?"

"A what?" I asked.

The Mexican lady replied, "It's a part of speech that provides a greater description to a verb or adjective."

So, there I was, 'my ignorance exposed', and from one minute to the next, I went from top of the class to dumb ass. The foreigners had of course learned grammar when they studied English, whereas I really don't remember learning it at all, many of us simply grow up with it.

Teaching Thai people was a challenge I was not prepared for. Thai students, in general, are rather timid and nervous about making mistakes and so reluctant to respond and get involved during lessons. The Thai education system does not provide for them to question, debate or disagree during lectures. In the Thai social status, the teacher comes in third place after royalty, grandparents, important elders and Buddhist monks, but above doctors and judges, given that they all have to be taught by teachers. This leaves the less confident students, shit scared of teachers because of their social importance. Police are ranked around the same level as taxi drivers, in fourth place!

The teaching course involved giving an English lesson once each week to classes of Thai students of different age groups. Not only has my writing become almost illegible over the years, I had never written on a white board at the front of a room, whilst explaining to those sitting in class behind me, so found it a very awkward experience. I would write my topics on the board and turn around to see a group of expressionless faces, staring into space. Trying to humour them was not always a good idea, as it was often met with polite smiles, deadpan faces and silence. Sometimes, however, it could be fun, after spelling out an item from the whiteboard, and teaching them the pronunciation. I would ask them to give me examples of something, such as, "What are your favourite foods?"

The responses would go something like…

"*Wostpok.*"

Me: "Wostpok, can you explain?"

"Yes, it's pig in cooking."

"Oh, you mean roast pork?"

"Yes."

"Wostpok,"

"*Plumps in tin.*"

"Can you describe?"

"Yes, fruit in tin."

"Oh, good one."

"Tinned plumbs?"

"Yes, plumps in tin."

And there was flog legs, teas on toast, crap legs, etc.

But in all respect, it was fun and so were the Thai students, once you gained their confidence. But truthfully, it was I that was learning and needed confidence.

At times, I thought what fun it would be to apply the teaching methods that I grew up with at my old school in Coventry, 'Barkers Butts', to the lessons. Stroll into the classroom, with a cane under my arm, strike it over a desk and shout out loud, "Pay attention." Scribble a load of waffle on the board and throw a board marker or eraser at any student I caught talking behind my back. Walk over to a student, ask them a question, and give them three seconds to answer, before shouting in their face, "Out with it, as the dentist said."

I learned, therefore, that teaching English to a class of foreign students is not my forte, although small group and one-on-one pronunciation and conversation is fun. I can get plenty of practice in that, chatting with foreigners I meet in Bangkok, and of course, with the bar girls.

So, what next? Maybe I should try and become an author!